Long Range Casting and Fishing Techniques

by
Paul Kerry

Beekay Publishers

Other angling titles by Beekay Publishers:

Sea
Dinghy Fishing at Sea by Phill Williams & Brian Douglas
Cod Fishing by John Rawle

Coarse
Carp Fever by Kevin Maddocks
Success with the Pole by Dickie Carr
Pike Fishing in the 80's by Neville Fickling
Basic Carp Fishing by Peter Mohan
Modern Specimen Hunting by Jim Gibbinson
Fishing for Big Chub by Peter Stone
Top Ten – Tactics for the major species from ten
leading specialist anglers. Edited by Bruce Vaughan
Redmire Pool by Kevin Clifford & Len Arbery
Tactics for Big Pike by Bill Chillingworth
Tiger Bay by Rob Maylin
In Pursuit of Carp & Catfish by Kevin Maddocks
Cypry The Carp by Peter Mohan
The Beekay Guide to 450 Carp Waters
Jim Davidson Gets Hooked by Jim Davidson
In Pursuit of Predatory Fish by Neville Fickling
Big-Water Carp by Jim Gibbinson

Game
The Colour Guide to Fly-tying by Kevin Hyatt
Robson's Guide – Stillwater Trout Flies. An
Alphabetical Survey in Colour by Kenneth Robson
Dressed to Kill by Bob Carnill & Kenneth Robson

(All titles available direct from Beekay – send for free catalogue)

British Library Cataloguing in Publication Data
Kerry Paul
    Long range casting and fishing techniques.
    1. Saltwater fishing
    I. Title
    799.1'6   SH457

First published 1984
Reprinted 1989

BEEKAY PUBLISHERS LTD.
Withy Pool, Henlow, Beds SG16 6EA
© PAUL KERRY 1984

Typeset and printed in Great Britain at The Bath Press, Avon.

ISBN 0 947674 03 9

Contents

All photography, including front and back covers, by John Wilson and Jim Oates.

Drawings by Jim Gibbinson.

Introduction

Over the years I have tried virtually every type of angling. Living in Norwich means that within twenty minutes I can be freshwater fishing on the Norfolk Broads or within thirty minutes fishing on the beach. It is a position that I am sure many anglers in other parts of the country would envy and it probably explains why a very high percentage of the local population indulge in one form of angling or the other. During my school days most of my time was spent freshwater fishing, mainly because of the lack of transport, but occasionally I would get the train to Great Yarmouth with a friend for a day's sea fishing. At that stage it only represented the chance to do something different rather than a deep desire to go sea fishing but once I left school and obtained my own transport the number of trips increased and so did the interest.

Right from those early days one particular point immediately became apparent and that was that the anglers who could cast well more often than not caught the most fish, or the biggest fish, or both. Naturally there were times when the opposite happened; the chap with the latest tackle, best casting style and huge baits caught nothing while the pensioner with cane rod, scraps of lugworm and 50 yard cast reeled in a double figure cod. These times were very rare though and taken over the season the angler who could cast would take a lot more fish than the pensioner and that's what really counted, not the freak catches.

Long distance casting from the shore is particularly successful on the fairly gently sloping beaches of East Anglia which offer only relatively shallow water. This is probably why casting in general is so popular there and why many of the country's top tournament casters live there. However one thing I would like to make perfectly clear and that is that virtually every one of those men are anglers first and casters second. Casting is only the means to an end and that end is to catch more and bigger fish not to show off to other anglers by continually putting baits out of sight.

East Anglians, particularly those living in Norfolk and Suffolk have been at the forefront of distance casting techniques, beach rod designs and more importantly distance fishing techniques to the extent that virtually all the generally accepted ideas and methods have originated from that area. That is not to say, of course, that there are not other good ideas or methods developed elsewhere because there are and other areas of the country have really top class anglers. No one with any sense is going to preach to a Geordie angler that he should use 15lb BS line in the kelp jungles of the north east or that the Scottish angler should learn to cast 150 yards plus with bait when he has fifty feet of water twenty yards from the rock ledges. The point to remember is that not all venues in the North East are kelp or in Scotland, deep. Other areas are very similar to the sandier beaches further south and could be potentially very good if exploited by anglers who cast well.

I am sure that part of the reason is that the fishing in East Anglia is centred mainly around one species and that is cod. These fish move inshore during late October or early November and stay until the end of April, so after that it is virtually a waste of time going. There are bass but after a few blanks most give up trying, thornbacks have been hammered by the commercial boys so that relatively few ever come within casting range and the millions of crabs reduce even the biggest baits to clean hooks in a matter of minutes, so everything centres on the winter and time has shown that distance counts. So, not only have you got to be a good all-round angler in terms of bait presentation and watercraft but you've then got to overcome the additional problems that long distance casting throws up. Reels that seem intent on over-running, baits that disintigrate, holding bottom in strong tide runs, hooking fish and actually mastering a technique that you can repeat cast after cast come fair weather or foul.

Learning to master these different aspects takes time and the apprenticeship is hard. One minute you seem to have it, everything is going perfectly then another disaster strikes. I have had times when I have wanted to throw everything in the sea and take up tiddly-winks, and only the cost of the tackle has stopped me. Eventually though you get there and the effort is more than repaid by the results. Days when you are one of the few anglers to catch fish, for example or the chance to fish beaches which are usually deserted because an inshore sand bar means that for the majority, the fish stay out of reach for all but a very small proportion of the tide.

Do not concentrate purely on the casting aspect because although it is probably the most important single one in some areas it must also be allied to the fishing aspect in most areas to make a really good angler. Most of the successful shore anglers in my area, where as I have said casting is very important, have a certain 'feel' for the fish they are trying to catch. It is a very difficult term to explain to the novice but I am sure the experienced anglers will know what I mean and it applies whatever type of fishing you prefer. This feeling allows you to pick the better beaches along the coast and then more specifically the better spots on that beach. You know which bait to have, at what time of year, what state of tide the fish feed best, which weather conditions they prefer and then finally how to present the bait and where to cast it to intercept the fish. Then with a bit of luck – and you always need a bit of luck – you will catch fish. If all those factors are right you will catch a lot of fish but more often than not one or more are not quite right and only a moderate catch results. The skill is getting as many of those factors as possible right and that is where experience helps. Unfortunately you cannot, as they say, put an old head on young shoulders and this experience only comes with time. It is not something that can easily be explained in words but I hope to provide enough information to cut out as much of the hard slog as possible forming good foundations on which to build.

You cannot possibly hope to concentrate on the finer points if every second or third cast results in a 'birds nest' or poor knots see the terminal tackle fly apart. Within these pages I hope that you will find the information to avoid many of the pitfalls that a majority of anglers are still struggling to overcome. Everything has been learnt either the hard way through experience or more easily from the numbers of very good casters and anglers it is my pleasure to know. Never worry about asking more experienced anglers for advice if you find yourself fishing next to one because most are only too willing to pass on their knowledge. Every chance of a short cut to better fishing should be taken.

Rods

A rod suitable for long range casting and fishing is probably the most important single item that the angler has to buy and is one that is surrounded by controversy. Although there are not many over-the-counter production rods that are suitable there is a vast range of blanks available all of which differ in length, taper, action, weight and price. Which one should you choose? Browse through any of the major angling publications and you will probably see numerous advertisements each trying to convince prospective customers that this is the right one for them. Often the adverts are accompanied by a photograph or statement telling how a monster fish was only landed because the angler was using their rod or some mind boggling distance was obtained using the latest super-duper blank. Usually the experienced anglers can see through them but for the novice it can be very confusing, he just doesn't have the experience to fall back on yet has to make some decision sooner or later. Let us then take a complete look at the surf rod scene and hopefully by explaining all the different points to consider some light will appear at the end of the tunnel.

Development

Many years ago catching fish from the sea and from freshwater was primarily for food and the sport aspect was nil. A handline was all that was really needed and even today a commercial fisherman using a handline could easily catch a lot more fish than a rod and line angler when working from a boat.

From the shore though it is certainly necessary to position a bait a reasonable way out and years ago this was comfortably done using a casting pole. Casting poles were very popular on the East Anglian coast and usually consisted of a broom handle with a nail hammered in the end to about half its length. The head of the nail was then filed smooth so that the line could slide off easily. The trace was usually a simple paternoster made up from fairly strong cord with a loop tied about five or six feet from the sinker. The loop was hung on the nail and then the trace cast out using a technique of facing away from the sea and throwing the sinker over the shoulder; a technique in fact which formed the basis of the 'Yarmouth' back-cast. The line was laid in a zig-zag pattern on the beach so without the friction of a reel to worry about quite

good distances could be obtained, certainly around the 100 yards mark by the more experienced 'pole' anglers.

The first rods were burma cane, or if you could afford them split cane, but both were very stiff and hardly encouraged sea angling as a sport. Even the first fibre glass models left much to be desired; solid glass was very soft in action and heavy in length of over ten feet so its main use was reserved for boat rods. Hollow glass blanks came shortly after and really started the trend towards light weight and more sporting sea rods. The trouble was that sea angling in general couldn't break out of the 'thick-eared' image and the new lightness image of the hollow glass was so impressive that little attention was paid to actions or overall rod power.

The first major break-through in producing a rod which could cast and fish well was the now legendary reverse taper design coupled with the layback cast. Leslie Moncrieff was the man responsible for this design and it consisted of a rod blank which tapered fairly slowly from the reel fitting to the tip and then tapered down again from the other side of the reel fitting to the butt cap. The rod gave a very smooth and even bend throughout its complete length (hence the name 'Longbow' from the Hardy company) and was supposed to take much of the jerkiness out of casting with a multiplier reel thereby reducing overruns. Leslie also practised what he preached; casting demonstrations throughout the country and massive hauls of cod from Dungeness proved the point.

The rods and casting style promoted by Leslie did much to contribute to better catches for a great many anglers during the sixties and created more interest in casting tournaments. The tackle trade was not slow to realise the market potential of good casting rods and in the late sixties ABU turned the beach fishing world upside down with the introduction of the fast taper, stiff-butt rod. With the new rod came new casting techniques – the pendulum cast developed by George Brown and Nigel Forrest who at the time were heavily involved with casting tournaments. This design of rod brought about the first 200 yard tournament casts and now distances in excess of 270 yards with rods which are very similar to those early models. Only the use of carbon fibre has changed the rods and that has really only given us lighter rods because the basic action is virtually the same. So that brings us up to date, although we are still in the stage of infancy with carbon fibre and progress will continue until another major break-through is achieved as I am sure it will be.

Selection

Before you are able finally to choose the rod you want a great many factors must be taken into consideration. Action, power, length, weight, positions of fittings such as reel clamps, hand grips, rings and the size of the rings must all carefully be considered so that they match your casting technique, physique, reel type and fishing location. That is quite a mixture so it is not surprising that many anglers get one or even more of them wrong causing them to struggle when really they shouldn't. Ideally it would be nice to try several different rods before you actually purchased one and some of the better tackle dealers will let you do this. For most, though, buying one is the only way to find out and with some carbon rods costing around the £100 mark it is an expensive lesson to get wrong.

Basically a surf rod should carry out three major functions; casting, bite detection and playing and landing a fish. The problem is of course designing a blank which does all these things perfectly, something that can't be done in reality and only a compromise can be reached. To cast well the rod has to have a certain amount of power which usually means stiffness, but to show bites well the tip must be fairly flexible. Also playing and landing fish requires a rod with a certain amount of stiffness so that you can exercise some control on a large fish yet it must retain enough flexibility to absorb any sudden lunges, especially when the fish reaches the breakers. Years ago it was virtually impossible to find a rod which held these qualities but modern ultra-fast and compound taper designs have managed to get as close as is realistically possible.

Considering the fact that the subject of this book is *long distance* shore fishing it is quite obvious that the casting aspect is the number one priority to consider. It must be remembered that all the bite sensitivity and fish playing ability in the world is absolutely useless if you can't reach them in the first place. Unfortunately a large number of anglers are of the opinion that a good casting rod is a massive super stiff 15 foot weapon and that certainly is not true. Of course a good casting rod does need a certain amount of stiffness and power but by good design it can be limited to certain areas of the blank. The other areas can be designed very much with fishing ability in mind to give the best of both worlds. In fact some of the very best casting rods have an incredible amount of flexibility making them excellent rods for fishing as well.

Rod Blanks

The slow taper glassfibre blanks used on beach-casting rods in the past, and unfortunately quite a few of today's production rods really are pretty useless when you consider the qualities necessary for a good casting/fishing rod. In a strong wind they would wave about in the rest making bite detection very difficult and under the pressures of hard casting they would completely fold-up. The result was a soggy, gut-less feeling and a very slow rate of recovery. You would go through the motions of the cast, release the line and then wait for what seemed like an age until the tip caught up, a kind of built in time delay which made you wonder if the tip would ever catch up.

Most modern blanks are however fast-actioned and have proved to be a considerable improvement in all respects. Basically they can be divided into three distinct sections (a) a fairly thin and flexible tip which gives good bite detection and absorbs the efforts of a fighting fish, (b) a moderately flexible middle section with enough muscle to cast lighter sinkers but enough 'give' to make the rod feel pleasant to use and (c) a very stiff and powerful lower section to really lever those heavier sinkers away. Each part then has its own particular job to do and the result is a rod that leaves the old slow taper designs miles behind. Obviously different blanks will vary in design, some tip sections may be a bit stiffer than others or some middle and bottom sections may have more muscle, generally though they follow the format mentioned. What you, the angler, have to do is to look closely at any blank and be sure that it will fulfil your requirements; the action, casting weight, casting style and reel type must all be considered. Just because a blank is best on the tournament court does not mean it is best on the beach and although competition casting improves the breed you usually find that something of a similar design but a bit less powerful makes a much nicer fishing/casting rod.

Glass Blanks

Compound Taper The first fast actioned blanks similar to the type used by ABU for the 484 were of a thick walled, compound taper like construction. For those of you not familiar with the term compound taper all it really means is a blank whose wall thickness varies along its length, quite often in distinct 'steps'. Although the overall look of the blank is of only a moderately fast taper the actual action of the blank is very fast. The tip section has a small diameter and the walls are quite thin giving flexibility, the walls then thicken for the middle section to stiffen it up a bit and the lower section is thickened up yet again to make it very stiff indeed. Compound taper blanks tend to show quite a distinct difference between the tip half of the blank and the lower half when compressed, making the recovery extremely fast indeed. Certainly the first anglers who switched to the 484 after their reverse taper rods were in for a shock. Their over-head thump casting style only bent the tip resulting in a very jerky cast and more often than not a massive 'birds nest' on the reel. A lot of 484's were sold but a large proportion ended up being sold second hand until better casting techniques became popularised.

Having thick walls compound blanks will take quite a lot of abuse both in handling and casting. Knocks on sharp edges really only result in a damaged finish and even if the glass is marked there is enough left undamaged to back it up. It is very rare to get a genuine breakage with compound blanks. Most of the blanks handle a wide range of sinkers, anything from 2–9 ounces which is very wide considering the very narrow 4–6 ounce or 6–8 ounce range of the old slow taper blanks. In reality, though, optimum performance still comes with a fairly narrow range usually in the 5–6 ounce area with about five and a quarter being perfect. It is reassuring to know that if the going really gets bad you can always step up sinker weight without over stressing the rod. The penalty, and there always is one, comes with excess weight. Because the walls are thick it means that quite a bit of material has to be used and even though glass fibre is basically quite light the finished blank still tends to be on the heavy side, especially if you like to hold your rod for long periods. All glass, compound taper blanks are fairly rare now mainly because the use of carbon fibre in rod making has enabled quite a bit of progress in this particular design, although I'll deal with that later. However they still make extremely good rods and if you get the chance to buy one of the old Conolon blanks at the right price you will have the basis of a first class rod.

Ultra-Fast Taper Blanks of this design came a few years after the compound models and much of the pioneering was done by the Carroll McManus company under the Conoflex name. As the description suggests the rate of taper from the butt end to the tip is extremely steep and the wall thickness of the

Compound taper

Ultra-fast taper

↖
carbon/glass mix

Semi-carbon

blank fairly thin. Even though the walls are not as thick as the compound blanks the strength comes from the extra diameter. That is not to say that some slight compounding isn't used because quite often it is, but the variation in wall thickness is nowhere near as marked.

The bonus of such a design is lighter weight but you do need to be much more careful in handling the blank. With thin walls excessive pressure can crush the glass or set up small hairline cracks. These may go unnoticed at the time but will soon show up after a hard cast, usually by a broken rod. I am sure that many so called 'breakages' that result in rods being taken back to dealers stem from careless handling. It is also much easier to over-stress the blank by using too heavy sinkers. The range is quite limited for good results and a 4–6 ounce limit would be typical.

The action of ultra-fast blanks is also slightly different from the compound type. The difference between the top half and the bottom half of the blank is not nearly as distinct. The action is more progressive which suits some styles of casting and reel types much better. Beginners often find this action more forgiving and easier to handle than compound blanks which tend to resemble a highly tuned engine; rough at low speeds but silky

smooth when flat out. Ultra-fast blanks seem to have a much wider power band because they still perform nicely at 'half throttle'.

Carbon Blanks

Carbon fibre has virtually taken over in the coarse and fly fishing world and now the talk is of Boron which is an even stiffer material. With surf rods the impact has been far less dramatic and although carbon was at first heralded as 'the' material the first attempts left much to be desired in terms of casting potential, fishing potential and price. Maybe it is still early days and more progress will be made but all indications are that it is a material that has its uses but only in certain areas of the blank.

Although carbon is very light it is also very stiff and all carbon rods show several disadvantages in use:

(a) Even with tip diameters kept very small they remain much stiffer than glass resulting in very poor bite detection.
(b) In heavy seas the breaking waves put a great deal of pressure onto the running line. A glass-fibre tip bends with the constant increase and

10

decrease in pressure absorbing most of it but the harder carbon is less sympathetic transmitting a lot of the pressure down the line to the sinker until it actually breaks free.

(c) Blanks made from 100% carbon seem to be either extremely stiff and virtually impossible to bend or more likely an all through action rather like the old glass blanks. The stiffer carbon certainly recovers much quicker but the action doesn't lend itself to distance casting techniques at all well.

So from both a casting and fishing aspect the all-carbon surf rod has not proved too succesful or popular. For some specialised applications where distance casting is not important and an all through action a positive advantage, such as surf or rock bassing at close range with soft baits, carbon has been used to produce some very good rods. Carbon also gives these lightweight rods a 'steeliness' that transmits the pulls and thumps of a fighting fish to the hands of the angler much more effectively than the more absorbing glass fibre. Therefore although the fish isn't actually fighting any harder it feels as though it is which for general fun is a good thing.

With the general range of shore fishing rods however it seems that the greater the emphasis placed on casting the greater the care needed in using carbon. To create rods which both cast and fish well the designers have had to think very carefully and now produce ranges of rods which come under the label of semi-carbons. Realising that they had to retain tip flexibility and sensitivity to maintain the rod's fishing performance yet keep the lower half of the blank very stiff for casting power most manufacturers only used carbon fibre in the lower two thirds of the blank. The top third is still pure glass and as you can imagine the area where the two materials meet must be carefully blended to avoid breakage. Early models were rather suspect in this area but now it is very rare that problems arise.

Although both the compound and ultra-fast taper blanks have received the carbon treatment it is the compound models which have benefited most. Blanks similar to the old ABU 484 and Conolon can now be made with considerably thinner walls and therefore much lighter yet be as stiff or even stiffer. The exact action will depend on how much carbon has been used and how far it has been 'pushed' up the blank. One semi-carbon rod I tried recently had only about fifteen inches of glass at the tip and acted rather like a stepped-up quiver tip used in coarse angling. When buying a compound semi-carbon it pays either to question the dealer about the amount of carbon used or place the butt end of the blank on the floor and then press on it fairly hard, at regular intervals along its length. This will give you some guide to the overall stiffness of the

blank because with some the casting aspect is catered for at the expense of the fishing aspect. How far you need to go will depend on just how much distance is a priority; if it is not, go for something with a bit more flexibility along the blank's length.

Ultra-fast taper blanks have also been altered in this manner and although the improvement has not been quite as marked it has allowed the production of blanks with a much wider range of actions. Even the glass ultra-fast blanks were not particularly heavy anyway so although they can now be produced even lighter the improvement is purely academic in most fishing situations. However this new generation of extremely light ultra-fast blanks has made its impact on the casting court with some notable distances being obtained by using them at lengths of thirteen feet plus along with the pendulum technique. Only a few years ago pendulum casting with rods this long was unthinkable; now a few are even being seen on the beach-but more of this later.

Two Piece or One? In tournaments it has been popular to use the blank of the rod in a single uncut length with the handle joined separately by means of a spigot. Indeed some blanks perform much better in one piece but others are virtually unaffected if they are cut. The general opinion is that a one piece blank has a better action but more often than not a blank that is cut and either spigotted or ferruled properly will virtually remain unaltered, at least as far as casting and fishing from the shore is concerned.

Certainly the heavy old brass ferrules added unnecessary weight and proved a nuisance when they stuck together, but modern spigots are very light and give virtually no trouble. With the compound taper blanks the walls tend to be fairly thick, even towards the middle of the blank where it is likely to be cut and therefore the hole up the centre is quite small. Any attempt to use a spigot on this design means that it will have to be virtually, or even totally, solid. Even so its size makes it a definite weak spot and with continuous hard casting it is likely to break.

Therefore the choice is a ferrule or one piece and quite honestly I would go for a one piece blank and separate handle. The only ferrule that I have ever rated was the one fitted to the ABU 484 and 464 rods. It was fairly light in weight, fitted together with just a hint of play to avoid sticking but could be locked solid by the threaded collar fitted. Other types fail miserably when compared with the ABU design.

Ultra-fast taper blanks on the other hand have a fairly large hole up the centre and adapt well to a spigot. This should be strong enough to take the stress and strain of hard casting and fishing but have enough give to let it flex slightly with the

blank. If it is too hard and rigid it may lever inside the blanks wearing away the material and eventually causing it to split. Even with a properly designed spigot the thin walls of the ultra-fast blanks need protecting by whipping the blank on either side of the joint by at least two inches. This applies equally to a one piece blank if it is joined to the handle by a spigot because the glass itself just can't stand the strain of casting unprotected.

Even if you keep the surfaces of the spigot clean it will eventually wear and the two edges will meet. Lubricating with wax can help to slow this process down and take up some of the slack but in the end all you can do is trim off the female section of the blank. These problems have to be weighed against the convenience of having a rod that breaks into shorter sections allowing much easier transportation and storage. For some of the longer types of rod the handle can be 5 feet long and it is hardly worth cutting the blank to give only a foot or so of glass onto it. With these it is more usual to leave the blank uncut. With rods of up to 12 feet, two equal sections are nice so although the ultimate performance does come from an uncut blank, for most applications a cut blank will perform well enough.

With two-piece blanks it is essential to whip both male and female sections to avoid splitting.

Handles

Moving down from the blank the next section of the rod is the handle or 'butt' as it is more usually called. Rod blanks have gone through quite a change over the years but so has the handle, even though it usually received only scant attention. The first glass rod builder simply put corks over the bottom three feet or so of the blank and that was it, but part of the Moncrieff theory was to use the butt to help the caster. From the reel fitting the blank tapered down towards the end cap; the 'reverse taper' it was called and the idea was to allow the handle to bend, thereby smoothing out the cast.

By bending though, the handle is absorbing much of the power being put into the cast by the angler. A rigid butt on the other hand transmits this power into the blank and a fast actioned tip needs butt rigidity to make it work. This was appreciated as soon as fast actioned rods came onto the market because most sported dural butts rather than the more conventional glass. It's absolutely useless to have a very powerful blank, which requires a developed casting technique to compress it successfully if the butt is absorbing much of the energy. Quite a few anglers found this out in past years, buying rods which, because a glass butt was fitted, never developed their full potential.

Rigidity therefore is essential and for a distance casting rod favoured materials are dural tubing, or ultimately, carbon. Dural has been used for many years and has been successfully used on the beach and the casting court. Its faults are that it is heavier than glass or carbon and is subject to corrosion if left exposed. The old 484's had a cork handle and screw winch fitting. The salt water would penetrate between the two and gradually eat away at the alloy, result – on a hard cast the butt snapped. On custom built rods most dealers covered the dural with shrink tube which meant a one piece covering and no gaps for the salt to get through.

Of course carbon is the ultimate not only in terms of performance but also unfortunately price. Length for length carbon costs about three times as much as dural. The advantages are lightness, which is quite considerable, resistance to corrosion and rigidity. The resistance to corrosion means that you don't need to be as careful to keep out the salt water as you do with dural but I still usually cover the handle with shrink-tube to save it from any harsh knocks. The rigidity factor is again most noticeable on longer rods but even in lengths of four feet you can notice a difference. Dural is quite a stiff material which bends gradually under pressure, the harder you cast the more it distorts until it actually takes a set. Mind you that stage is rarely reached if you use good quality stuff such as HT or aircraft spec. Avoid the lower grades such as HE because they do bend quite easily. Carbon on the other hand bends slightly to begin with then 'locks up'; it just won't bend any more no matter how hard you cast. So, even more energy is transferred to the blank and on the tournament court a few more yards could be gained. On the beach though the difference really is hardly worth worrying about. At one time I was using two identical tips; one with a dural handle, one with a carbon handle. After a cast you could always tell which was which because the carbon felt much more taut but in terms of distance the difference was negligible.

For most fishing applications where the rod spends most of its time in the rest and absolute distance is not necessary dural is good enough and considerably cheaper. A carbon butt is a luxury really which improves the feel of the rod.

Much depends on how much you want to spend so don't be led to believe that carbon will make an average caster into a good caster because it will not and that applies equally to the blanks as the handles.

Rod Fittings Traditionally, sea rods have been equipped with a heavy chromed brass screw winch fitting to hold the reel. It was considered necessary from a resistance to corrosion viewpoint and because of the strain it had to withstand during fishing. In recent years though new lightweight designs have appeared and rod handles have been stripped of superflous weight to reveal a 'tournament' type style.

A length of shrink-tube, a rubber button on the end and the reel fitting are all that are necessary really with a couple of rubber or leather hand grips added purely for comfort. The new generation of screw-winch fittings are made in plastics and light alloys and are equally as durable as the old brass versions. Fuji of Japan produce a range that fits most diameters of handle. All they need is to be glued in position so make sure you place the fitting exactly where you want it and also make sure that there are no gaps between the fitting and the handle covering, otherwise the previously mentioned corrosion will set in with an alloy handle.

Another very popular fitting is the stainless steel sliding type by Fuji. These are very light in weight and because they are whipped or taped on have the advantage that you can try various positions of the

Modern reel fittings. Top to bottom – the FPS screw winch type, the sliding snap-lock, hose-clips or 'coasters'.

reel without the need for a major handle rebuild. The only comments I have on sliding fittings is that for hard casting they do not hold multipliers quite as securely as I would like. No matter how hard you clamp the reel it always seems to work slightly loose, not enough for the reel to be in danger of dropping out but enough to be annoying. The way the fitting is positioned can be important also. Most photographs, or actual rods I have seen, show the fitting with the sliding part uppermost. However, experience has shown that with a multiplier reel the hand gripping the spool tends to push against the reel during casting, forcing the sliding part of the fitting out of its locking grooves. The catch may move only a couple of grooves but it makes the reel quite loose, an annoying thing every time you cast. With fixed-spool reels I have found that the line sometimes hooks around the catch holding the sliding part when you release it to cast. The result is a cut line and lost tackle so with both multiplier and fixed-spool reels I prefer to position the fitting so that the sliding part is beneath the reel rather than above. You can buy the sliding fitting already fitted to a tube which is then glued to the handle in the same way as the screw winch type. The same problems apply through, exact positioning is a must and also care against corrosion. Personally I prefer to whip or tape mine so that the shrink tube is continuous and the fitting can be removed easily.

My own favourite and that of many pendulum

'Coaster' fittings are very popular with multiplier casters because the index finger can be wrapped around it in a similar manner as a trigger.

Modern rod rings. Left to right – chromed wire, Daiwa Dynaflow, Seymo Dynalite, Fuji BNHG, Fuji HG.

casters is to use the hose type fittings or 'coasters' as they are known. These fittings enable the reel to be placed anywhere along a shrink-tube covered handle although their design means that they are really only suitable for use with multipliers. I particularly like the fact that when gripping the reel the first finger naturally wraps around the clip as if it was a 'trigger'. This gives a much firmer and tighter grip on the spool and on the rod in general during casting. It's something that is very reassuring and certainly helps you to hit the rod that bit harder along with greater confidence. The clips do have very sharp edges and a crack-off in mid cast can result in a cut finger. To avoid this I cut a short piece of rubber tube and slide it over the clip thereby cushioning any sudden pressures.

With the screw-winch and sliding reel fittings you can whip your own trigger onto the handle. I have seen a Fuji screw-winch fitting complete with a trigger in a tackle catalogue but unfortunately they do not seem to be generally available in the shops. I managed to obtain some light weight fittings from a shop dealing in boat equipment. These are ideally suited to whipping onto the handle because they are shaped to be fitted onto a circular material and although the 'hooked' part is bent over more than required it is soft enough to be bent out slightly to the right shape.

Rings The purpose of rod rings on a blank is to guide the line and for distances of about 150 yards with a lead alone just about any set-up will do. However, above this figure the frictional forces become much greater and require that more attention be paid to the size and positioning of the rings. From the fishing point of view good quality durable rings are a must and spending that bit extra usually pays off in the long run. Nothing is more frustrating

than whipping on a new set of rings only to find that they break with the slightest provocation or groove after only half a season's use.

A few years ago the choice of rod rings was very limited; the major types used by major manufacturers and amateur rod builders were chromed wire or wire formed with a porcelain insert. The latter were not quite so popular due to the fact that they are rather heavy which could spoil the action of the rod and the inserts did not stand up to knocks very well. Most of the better quality rods had wire rings which were very light and fairly cheap. Problems were that the soldered frames would break or the ring actually squash up under pressure when rods were jammed into holdalls or bundled into the car. Also their life expectancy in use wasn't too long, the constant sawing action of the line causing grooving especially on those nearest the tip where the pressure is greatest.

Now there is quite a wide selection of rings and probably most popular are the new breed of ceramic lined rings. Their design is completely different from the old type of ceramic rings featuring a metal frame surrounding a luminous plastic shock absorber and finally very hard oxide liners which are virtually ungroovable. The frames come in three styles, a standard four legged cradle, a three legged cradle and a single leg. The latter have proved very popular on fly rods so that the natural bend of the blank is maintained as far as possible but the single whipping makes them suspect for surf rod use. Under the constant strains of casting, retrieving and general handling I feel that they would quickly loosen and move out of alignment, or perhaps even fall off.

Even the standard four legged cradle will twist under really hard casting because the rings do tend to stand well away from the blank. Therefore they are subject to a fair amount of leverage so although the seat may be firmly whipped to the blank the frame just twists over. The problem becomes greater with fewer rings because there are less to take the strain. The modern fixed-spool set-ups show this problem particularly well because they use only three to four rings and therefore the large Fuji ceramic rings which feature a much stronger frame than standard are usually used. For multiplier reels I favour the three-leg type because they are very tough, taking hard knocks and general abuse and will resist grooving for years.

That doesn't mean to say that steel rings are not worth considering because the new Daiwa Dynaflo range have taken over from the plain chromed wire. They are very light indeed featuring a four-leg frame and polished steel liner although their newness on the market means that their grooving resistance has still to be established. Being very cheap when compared with ceramic rings is also a plus point.

An area where I do find steel rings best is on the tip. Certainly not the tungsten carbide type though because although they are hard they are also very brittle. They shatter at the slightest knock on a rock or shingle and as most people tend to drop their rod every now and then it could mean a successful session suddenly comes to an end. You can usually struggle through with a broken intermediate but a broken tip makes casting virtually impossible. The best type are the Diamite tip rings which are smooth and although they will eventually mark, it takes several seasons of very hard use before they need replacing. The trouble with the ceramic rings is that although they work superbly as intermediates where the main line runs across them fairly flatly, even when the blank is flexed, they tend to 'bite the line' when used on the tip. Because the

Leader knots catching in the frame of the first ring can be a problem at times with fixed-spool reels. Wrapping it with tape, as shown, can help.

line is pulled sharply across them it creates considerable resistance showing up particularly badly when the rings are dry on a warm sunny day. It is surprising really but you can feel it as you reel in and I found that the problem was much reduced by fitting a Diamite tip ring. With the set-up for fixed spool reels the only tip ring available of the right size is ceramic so unfortunately there is no choice for those anglers wanting casting performance with this type of reel.

The Complete Rod

Having looked at all the separate components that go to make a shorefishing rod I want to put them together to form the complete item. The major influences on which ones to choose are (a) the casting style and (b) the reel type. Many anglers tend to wander along to their local tackle shop intent on buying a fast taper rod, convinced that it will be the passport to success. His choice may already be made up having been influenced by an advertisement in the angling press, or perhaps it will be made for him by the dealer. This is all right if the dealer knows his stuff but a great number don't so it pays to have a reasonable idea of the type of rod you are looking for. A good rod could cost as much as £100, so you want to ensure the best value possible in terms of pleasure and results.

Pendulum Rods For most sea anglers a typical shore fishing rod measures between eleven and twelve feet. Tradition has probably played a major part in this opinion but so has general ease of handling and casting for Mr. Average. The many problems encountered on the shore, steep shingle, uneven rocks, soft sand and strong swells that come rushing up the beach mean that long rods can become heavy and unwieldy. This is particularly true if the reel is mounted at the bottom of the handle as some casting techniques require it to be. Personally I prefer a rod between these limits because it is so adaptable to all kinds of venues in all kinds of conditions; the same cannot be said for all set-ups.

Whether you use fixed-spool or multiplier reels the most successful length is in the 11 ft 6 inch to 11 ft 10 inch range. Pendulum casting relies on moving the rod very quickly for distance and once you start getting above 11 ft 10 inch and certainly 12 ft the leverage starts working against you instead of for you. This is with sinkers in the 5–6 oz range; above that the rod length should be even less although there are not many conditions that can't be mastered with 6 oz. As long as the overall length is within these limits then it doesn't really matter what it is exactly, the odd inch or two may make a couple of yards difference to you personally to suit your build but it is not going to give you twenty yards just like that.

However, reel type is important when choosing the rod's action. Multipliers can be used successfully on either compound or ultra-fast taper blanks but the very best results come with the compound taper, particularly the semi-carbons. The soft tip/stiff bottom combination seems to be just right, the tip bending easily at the start of the cast making the rod feel easy and pleasant to cast and the bottom giving the rigidity to lever the lead away. Because the tip bends easily it shortens the effective length of the rod which then allows it to be moved very quickly through the final stages of the cast.

Most compound blanks are very fast in action

A fast actioned rod under compression showing the soft tip/stiff bottom parts of the blank clearly.

COMPARISON OF EFFECTIVE LENGTHS OF ULTRA-FAST AND COMPOUND TAPER BLANKS

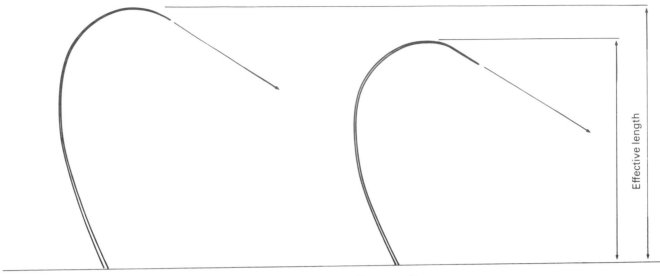

Ultra-fast taper

Compound taper

Blank shape under compression. Very flexible tip of compound taper blank bends more than ultra-fast blank resulting in shorter effective length therefore allowing rod to be moved very quickly for conventional pendulum cast

and give best results when worked hard. For the novice it may pay to start off with a fairly mild ultra-fast taper blank which will still be capable of very respectable distances but allow that bit extra time in the cast to sort yourself out. In fact some casters do prefer the ultra-fast blank's action and just move up to one that has a bit more power in the lower half, probably an ultra-fast semi-carbon. It is noticeable though that the majority still prefer the very fast compound blanks for multipliers and that's the type I would recommend.

The rings can be kept fairly small and therefore light to maintain the rod's action. Whichever type you finally choose, space them mainly near the tip of the rod because this is the area where it bends most. Also keep the first ring well away from the reel because with multipliers the line is thrown off in a bow like shape, funneled by the first ring. The closer the ring is to the rod the more it will choke the line's flow causing excessive friction and increasing the possibility of the leader knot catching. About seven rings should be enough to keep the line clear of the blank although some manufacturers seem intent on filling every few inches with rings – perhaps they feel it helps justify the price!

With fixed-spool reels a totally different set-up is necessary. The very tip actioned compound taper blanks just don't seem to work very well with this type of reel for two main reasons. Firstly, to get the very best results in terms of distance the rings need to be quite large in diameter which also unfortunately means that they are heavy. This makes the tip half of the blank feel really sloppy and contri-

butes to the second problem; because it is so flexible it twists round very badly as the cast is made often resulting in the leader wrapping around the rings and cracking off. Considering fixed-spools are supposed to be trouble free, losing terminal tackle in this matter can be very annoying.

Therefore to support the rings and reduce the chances of tangling, the slightly stiffer tip half and more 'through' action of the ultra-fast taper blanks seems to be much more successful. You can still use the semi-carbon type because although the carbon stiffens the lower half for better casting the tip retains enough stiffness to avoid problems, never really reaching the dramatic difference in tip half to bottom half that is a feature of the compound taper blanks.

The cause of much of the problem, the rings, need careful selection because they can affect potential distance to a far greater degree than on multiplier rods where virtually anything within reason is acceptable. With fixed-spool reels the line leaves the reel in large coils travelling up the rod at high speeds. Therefore anything they come into contact with, i.e. the rings, is going to cause friction and friction cuts distance. It is obvious then that these large coils are going to find it a tight squeeze to get through a small diameter opening so the rings need to be very wide and placed as far away from the spool as is practicable. Try casting hard with a rod equipped with small rings; the friction of the line as the lead hurtles away is almost enough to drag it out of your hands.

As far as actual sizes are concerned the practical

REEL AND RING POSITIONS ON PENDULUM RODS

Overall rod length 11½–12 ft (all ring/reel spacings in cm)

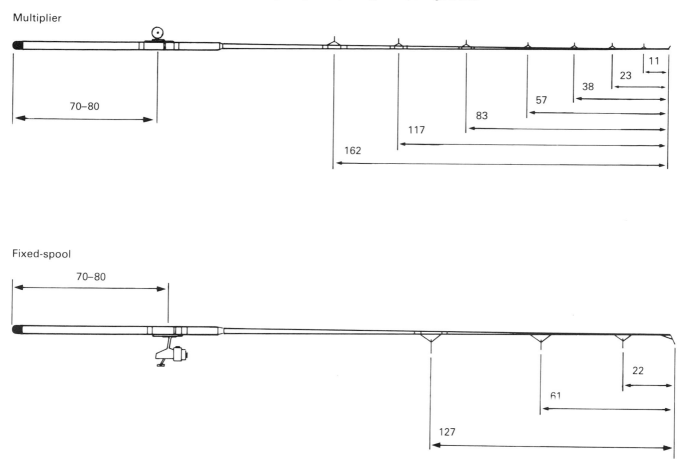

aspect becomes important because rings that are too big will just be a general nuisance and vulnerable to damage. The popular tournament set-up and that used by many long range shore anglers is to use only three intermediate rings and a tip. From the fishing angle you may prefer to use four with only a very slight drop in distance although I personally use only three and have never felt the need to use any more. However, you do need to be careful of the type you use because even though there are many designs available which are wide many are let down by the fact that the frames are just not strong enough.

With pendulum casting the rings do not stay in the same plane relative to the blank throughout the cast and during the period that maximum power is applied they receive a terrific sideways pull. Because there are so few rings the strain on each ring is considerable and this will try to pull them out of alignment. I have had rings actually end up 180° out of alignment and had to resort to either glueing them in position before whipping, or double whipping very tightly. Even with the seats rigidly fixed any ring with a slightly flimsy frame will find itself bent out of line and therefore a very strong frame is

a must. The best I have found are the ceramic Fuji rings which have a very strong frame and although slightly on the heavy side never move once properly fixed. Three of these plus a tip ring positioned well away from the reel reduce friction and give as good a fishing and casting performance as can reasonably be expected from a fixed-spool reel.

Although I favour the 11 ft 6 inch – 11 ft 10 inch rod for general long range casting/fishing work there has, as I mentioned earlier, been a trend towards using much longer rods. These are often over 13 ft in length and although they can prove unwieldy it would not be fair to omit them especially as some anglers have found them a considerable advantage distance wise.

The most popular blanks are the ultra-fast semi-carbons because of their action and very light weight, the latter being very noticeable on such a long rod. Again the compound taper types, even the semi-carbons don't seem to have the right action and are often a bit too heavy anyway. The long rod slows the whole casting action down allowing the caster more time to sort himself out, a point that appeals to many. Because the rod is that much longer the final tip speed can be equal to that

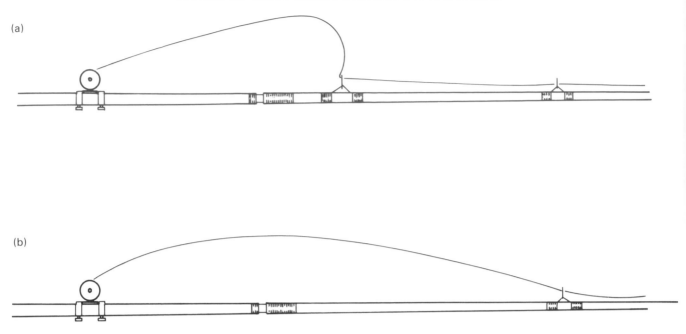

(a) Line emerging at high speed forms a bow in line which is
choked by first ring being too close to reel

(b) With ring further away line has a chance to smooth out

of the shorter rod although it is noticable that the better tournament casters using this set-up are all of above average strength. The leverage against the caster is high and you do need a fair bit of strength to maintain reasonable tip speed. Not my cup of tea personally for all round casting/fishing efficiency but a set-up that is increasing in popularity where distance is absolutely vital.

To aid casting with these longer rods the reel is usually mounted at the lower end of the butt to help balance the tip. This can also be done on the shorter rods but does not give much advantage, if any, over the more conventional upper position. In fact from the fishing point of view it is a positive nuisance resulting in the reel getting swamped with salt water or filled with sand unless you are very careful. There is no doubt that reels mounted in the lower position certainly take some hammer. Reeling in is also very difficult because there is very little of the handle protruding past the reel to tuck under your arm. Add to the situation a struggling double figure cod in a rough sea and by the time you actually beach it your arm will be fit to drop off.

Taking all circumstances into account I think that the higher reel position is better but whichever way round you choose one thing that is very important is hand spacing. In theory the closer together you have your hands on the handle the faster you would be able to punch the rod at the final part of the cast. Therefore with a long rod and very close hand spacing the tip speed would be absolutely

fantastic. In practice of course this just doesn't work because the leverage working against you would make it virtually impossible for the average person to move fast enough. By shortening the rod length and/or increasing the hand spacing casting is that much easier but you must not increase it too much. The old reverse taper rods had the reels mounted 35–40 inches up the handle because the layback style relied on power being produced by the top hand, the bottom hand acting as a tether for the butt thereby contributing almost nothing to the cast.

With modern pendulum techniques both hands contribute to the cast using a punch-pull movement to whip the tip over. Therefore a spacing is reached which is just right being neither too short or too long and for the average person this is usually about shoulder width apart, say approximately 25–30 inches. A good way to start is to place the butt cap in your arm-pit and then stretch your arm out along the handle with the reel being positioned so that the spool rests under your thumb. This will give a position that will be good enough to learn the basis of the cast and then you may like to try altering it a fraction to see which spacing suits you best. That's the beauty of sliding reel fittings – they can be altered to any position.

Back-Casting Rods Although back-casting is a much less popular casting technique compared with pendulum casting if you take the country as a

20

whole it is still very popular in tournaments and very successful for some fishing locations. One of the reasons that it has failed to catch on is probably the very long rods that are used. This is usually about 13 ft 6 in – 14 ft 6 in and a rod of this length that probably includes a handle of 1¼ inches diameter looks a mighty weapon.

Obviously a suitable blank needs to be fairly light so that the rod is not tip heavy and therefore the thick walled compound taper blanks are not widely used. Their weight is not the only reason because the action of these blanks, with the soft, flexible tip does not suit this technique which relies on leverage for distance. Although compound blanks can be very stiff in the lower half, on an 11 ft 6 in rod mounted on a long handle they feel quite soft. Far better results come from the ultra-fast taper blanks because they are light and have a more progressive action; the lower half is slightly softer and the tip half slightly stiffer. That is not to say that the action is not fast or in the tip because as discussed in the *Blanks* section it is, but once under compression the two blanks behave in different ways which is why it is so important to match the right one to your casting style or in the case of pendulum casting, reel type. Luckily with back-casting rods the one type of blank suits fixed-spool reels and multipliers equally well.

A very interesting point is that the semi-carbon ultra-fast blanks have made much less difference to the ultimate distance obtainable than was at first thought. Although tournament casters have squeezed a few extra yards out of them it is debatable if it is the rod or just better casting. Certainly from a fishing viewpoint a pure glass blank would prove more than adequate in all respects.

Much the same can be said for the handle. With blanks measuring around eight feet long that leaves quite a length for the butt and of course glass fibre is out because of its flexibility. Popular for many years has been the good old dural tubing usually at least 1⅛" O.D. and more often 1¼" O.D. Dural is fairly rigid in these lengths, reasonably light and quite cheap. A carbon butt would offer more rigidity but again the distance increase would probably only be noticable over grass and the cost is very high, a 5 ft 6 in length being about £50. Naturally it is much lighter but although this is certainly an advantage on the long pendulum rods the same has not proved true with back-casting rods. The carbon handles have in fact proved too light, making the tips feel heavy and the whole rod badly balanced. Dural on the other hand is not too heavy but heavy enough to balance the tip making the rod feel much better and nicer to use. Considering many of the top tournament casters who use this style stick to dural it must represent a good recommendation for the caster/fisherman to do the same.

Fast actioned rods with a more even bend throughout their length work best for back-casting.

Reels are mounted at the bottom of the handle and that is really the only place for them. The end of the handle is placed in the stomach throughout the cast and the lower hand simply holds it there and controls the reel. The upper hand simply sweeps the rod through the casting arc and its position is much easier to arrive at. The highest that it can be is the length of your arm – because you can't stretch any further and you will find that it will naturally settle in the place that feels most comfortable. Reeling in is not very comfortable with multipliers because of the reasons mentioned in the section on long pendulum rods but with a fixed-spool the upper hand can be positioned well up the butt to support the weight of the rod and leverage from any fish. In fact fixed-spool reels are very pleasant to use with long rods when they are mounted at the lower end of the handle for both casting and fishing, something I wouldn't say about multipliers.

Much of the casting advantage with long rods and fixed-spool reels is the fact that the reel can be positioned well away from the first ring. Although the rings should be approximately the same size as

Overall rod length 13 to 14½ ft (all ring/reel spacings in cm)

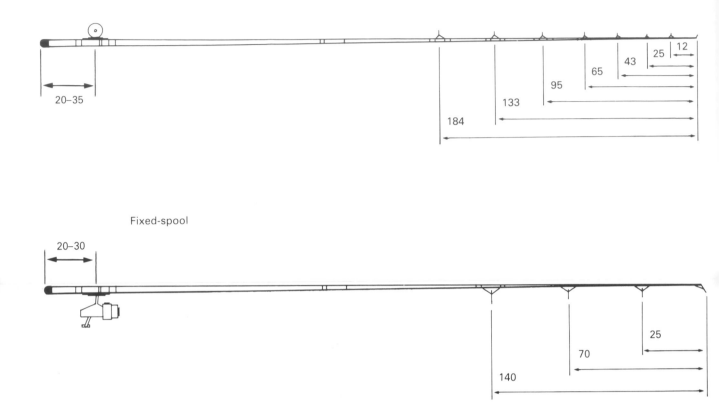

Multiplier

Fixed-spool

the short pendulum rods they allow the coils coming off the spool time to straighten out slightly before reaching them. This appears to be proven on the tournament court by the fact that the better fixed-spool casters often use the back-cast yet haven't the same advantage with multiplier reels.

The type of rings can also be the very strong Fuji ceramics but the different style of casting does not seem to put the same side-ways strain on them and therefore some of the many other designs can be used. As long as the centre is wide enough they should be all right. A set of multiplier rings can be any design you fancy although it pays to look for a set with good durability and also they can be spread out over more of the blank. Not being quite so flexible in the tip there is no need to push them quite so close to that end with ultra-fast blanks. A final point with back-casting rods is to fit a well rounded rubber button onto the end of the handle. This is because it sits tightly in the stomach during

both casting and reeling in which could prove uncomfortable with a small blunt button.

So that covers the types of rod currently favoured for both casting and long range fishing. Each has its advantages and disadvantages but for all-round fishing efficiency I don't think you will beat the 11 ft 6 in – 12 ft pendulum rods and casting style. The longer pendulum rods are now very light but are nowhere near as adaptable. Both these and the back-casting rods need room to use effectively and work best on moderately sloping sand/shingle beaches where there is space and the water is not likely to be surfing in from any distance. However, some anglers have found better distance with longer rods used pendulum style and sinkers in excess of 6 oz are certainly handled better by back-casting. If therefore you feel that you local terrain would be more easily conquered with these types of rods by all means choose one but if not stick to the more conventional lengths.

Reels

The second item on the agenda for a casting/ fishing outfit is a reel. Years ago there was only one choice and that was the basic revolving drum or 'centrepin' as it was known. Control of these reels was very difficult with a better than average chance of getting your knuckles rapped from the fast revolving handles, but some of the more proficient users could put baits out to the 100 yd mark. A modification on the revolving drum came from the side-cast reel which had its roots in Australia. The reel basically resembled the ordinary centre-pin but for casting the spool was turned to face forwards, the line peeling off as a conventional fixed-spool. The spool was then turned back for reeling in but by casting like a fixed-spool and reeling in as a centrepin terrible line twist was caused and therefore the side-cast never really caught on in a big way.

The big steps forward came with the introduction of the multiplying reel and proper fixed-spool, both adding a new dimension to sea angling. The first multipliers came from America where they had already proved very popular and since that time modern materials and technology have improved them considerably. Fixed-spools have also been improved but the progress has not been as rapid as it could have been. Part of the trouble I am sure is that fixed-spools have always been thought of as a reel for the novice and therefore the pressure on the major manufacturers has not been there to push them to produce something really first class. Even today with the use of finer lines which allow the fixed-spool to compete very favourably with the multiplier for distance there still is not one which I would say is perfect. I'm sure if there was though it would absolutely sweep the others out of contention.

Multiplier or Fixed-Spool? How they perform

The arguments as to which of these two reels is best have been discussed by anglers since their introduction on to the British market and even to this day nobody can really say that one is totally superior to the other. As with a shore fishing rod, a reel has certain tasks to perform and these are a) To store enough line b) To allow it to be cast off in a reasonably controlled manner c) To wind it back again against the pressure of a fish or heavy weed. As long as these are carried out efficiently then really any reel that does them ought to be good enough and both multiplier and fixed-spool reels

certainly will. It is only when you become very critical, such as exercising personal preferences, that small faults and flaws show up. However these do not detract from the fact that for practical fishing either reel is suitable.

Firstly then the reel must hold enough line of the appropriate breaking strain with strain being the word with nylon lines. Reeling in a large fish or more particularly heavy weed will cause nylon to stretch and the thinner the line the greater the stretch. This will result in the line going onto the spool under tension and as the line is built up, so the pressure increases up to a level measurable in tons per square inch. Obviously the spool will have to be very strong indeed to resist this level of pressure and some of the cheaper reels fitted with a plastic spool will shatter. On some it could be dramatic enough to force the end plates off a multiplier or cause the front of a fixed-spool to drop off leaving a heap of line on the floor. By careful design and the use of good materials such as lightweight alloy or special nylon/fibreglass mixtures, the spool can withstand these forces but even so they cannot be neglected if you want long and trouble-free life. It pays therefore to remove the line after every couple of trips or so and rewind it under less tension, thereby avoiding any build up of pressure.

Spool capacity should be enough to handle your own fishing situation. Most distance venues tend to be fairly snag free and therefore lines of up to 0.4 mm diameter (18 lb BS) should be ample. To handle casts of 150 yds plus you will need about 220 yds of line so therefore a spool with an ultimate capacity of 250 yds would be about right. Most of the fish you are likely to contact around the British coastline are not likely to strip vast quantities of line off the reel unless you are a tope fanatic. Then, with the possibility of 100 yd runs, you will need a spool with the capacity for a good cast plus enough to handle a run of this length. Lower capacity spools are easier to control from a casting point of view but there is no point in using one if you are going to lose the fish everytime and of course there is no point using a large capacity reel if you only ever use a third of the line on it.

Secondly it must be cast off in a reasonably controlled manner. Fixed-spool and multiplier reels each pay out line in a totally different fashion and each has its inherent advantages and disadvantages. On the tournament court there is approximately fifteen yards between the maximum distances of each type of reel with the multiplier being the one in front. On the beach however where conditions are not always very favourable and there is the additional resistance of baits and spiked sinkers to cut even more yards off the cast, there is very little difference at all. Certainly that is the case with a main line of around 0.35 mm diameter (15 lb BS) and should line technology improve to the degree that the same breaking strain can be made in lines of only 0.30 mm or even less then the fixed-spool may move ahead. Multipliers also benefit from finer lines but the advantage is not as great as it is with fixed-spools. Above 0.4 mm diameter (18 lb BS) the multiplier is certainly better and although they have always been considered so because of their tournament results for practical fishing/casting applications either type can be used.

The multiplier pays out line from a revolving drum and is well known for the problem of overruns. Many anglers are automatically put off buying one from this point of view and this is probably the reason that fixed-spools out sell multipliers.

By learning to cast smoothly and using a good quality multiplier equipped with a centrifugal breaking system, or more lately a magnetic control, overruns can be reduced to a very rare event indeed. You will never totally eliminate them, because even the best casters have that odd mishap but by setting the reel up according to ability I would say that it is possible to make a multiplier even more trouble free than a fixed-spool. Some of the older and cheaper multipliers which are not fitted with controls can be hard to use, but even these can be tamed once you know how to set them up which I'll be dealing with later. Generally it pays to buy a good quality reel and although this is likely to be over £40, unless you can get hold of a good second hand one, it is worth it for trouble free use and long life.

With fixed-spools the line comes off the spool in coils. Unless you drastically overfill the spool causing the line to come off in tangles, or 'bunches' you should not have any problems with control. Underfilling the spool will only cause a loss in distance because of excessive friction at the spool lip, not trouble in control and although the need of correct line level is always 'hammered' both to sea and freshwater fixed-spool users it's surprising how many under-filled spools you still see.

Fixed-spool reels are supposed to be much easier to use although this can usually be translated to mean that an angler will get into less trouble with a fixed-spool if he casts badly than he would by using a multiplier. That certainly can be true and although there is no excuse for not learning to cast properly I have seen anglers trying desperately to pendulum cast, doing it all wrong, yet managing a respectable distance and catching a few fish. The casting action has been ragged,

jerky and certainly a disaster would happen with a multiplier but the fixed-spool has allowed them to get away with it. In the long term their fishing will never reach a very high standard but at least their bait is in the water and still attached to the reel. Considering many of them either don't have the time or just don't want to learn to cast then they have made the best choice and if you feel in the same frame of mind then that is the reel for you. Problems do still arise though and one of the main and most annoying one is that the loops of line will catch around a ring or the rod tip every now and then. The result of this is usually a set of terminal tackle sent flying out to sea unattached and surprisingly the problem doesn't reduce with smooth casting. In tournaments where the rod is really hit hard this problem causes more crack-offs than does overruns in the multiplier events.

Thirdly then, the reel must be able to retrieve the line plus whatever happens to be hanging on the end, hopefully a big fish but more likely weed. Not only must it be retrieved but in a manner that will allow the next cast to be made without any problems. On a fixed-spool the line is distributed across the spool by the bale arm and the profile the line assumes is controlled by the manner in which the internal gearing moves the spool up and down. Usually the better the quality of the reel the more thought will have gone into gearing design and the more evenly the line will be laid on. That is not always the case of course but many cheaper models are hopeless in this respect leaving gaps at either the back or the front of the spool or even both. The result is that the line being wound in under tension slips into these gaps and can become caught up thereby reducing distance on the next cast.

With multipliers the way that the line is laid onto the spool is very important and it must be level over the complete width. Some models come complete with a level wind mechanism built in to do the job for you but the disadvantages greatly outweigh the advantages from a long range casting/fishing point of view. Most levelwinds tend to move across the spool far too quickly distributing the line in a criss-cross fashion rather in a better, much tighter, cotton reel fashion. Without the coils being packed tightly together the overall spool capacity is much reduced, some models quoting a capacity of around 220 yds of 0.4 mm line with level-wind yet without it you can comfortably get on 250 yds. Other hazards are that sand soon clogs the gearing of levelwinds in windy weather possibly resulting in it jamming up completely, not very good just as that fish reaches the breakers. Also in the event of you being unfortunate enough to get an overrun it is much more difficult to get at the spool to pick it out and if the line has broken the mechanism needs to be re-syncronised with the line position. Many of the better quality reels come with levelwinds particularly the small baitcasting size that are currently very popular with both tournament casters and distance beach men. It is noticeable that the first thing they do is to modify the reel taking out the level wind completely.

Also concerning the retrieving process both fixed-spool and multiplier reels come equipped with a clutch mechanism and although dabs and whiting are not likely to rush around stripping line off, when the need to give line does arise you want the clutch to do it smoothly and quickly. Many anglers totally overlook this vital part of the reel until the line snaps that is – and then examine its setting, assuming that it has not siezed up through neglect. Even though large cod and bass are not really great fighters the danger time is when they reach the area just behind the breaking waves. In heavy seas a receding wave will set up a very strong undertow which can pick the fish up and sweep it, suddenly, ten yards or more back out to sea. At this point the clutch must operate smoothly and give as much line as required without sticking. Too much pressure and a weak hook hold will give way or the hook straighten, leaving you with another story of the big one that got away.

Most multipliers have acceptable clutches which operate smoothly over a range of settings from totally free to fully locked. I usually set mine onto a very hard setting and by standing away from the water's edge I can absorb any sudden lunges on the rod tip by moving closer to the water. Then, as the fish comes closer to the danger zone I slacken it off ready for that powerful surge. Obviously if you are fishing for tope which make a run for freedom as soon as the hook goes in you will have to set it straight away, but for most average fish the first technique works well enough.

Unfortunately the picture with fixed-spool reels is not as rosy. Clutch mechanisms on these reels usually vary from poor to terrible and part of the problem seems to come at the bail arm roller where the lines makes a sharp angle, causing considerable friction. If the setting is too high the pull necessary to get the clutch working will break the line although once it is actually moving it is fine. Set it so that it gives line and it is usually slipping at the slightet excuse which won't do either. It's a problem that the manufacturers cannot seem to overcome successfully, because I feel, the line has to go through that 90° angle around the roller. Also for hard casting the clutch has to be screwed down very tightly otherwise it will allow the spool to turn and the line cut through your finger! That means you are for ever adjusting it and many anglers in my area tend to leave it screwed hard down all the time and back wind if they need

to give line. That does away with any worries about how well or otherwise the clutch operates!

That I hope gives you some idea of how the reels operate and which you choose is up to your personal preference. Many anglers just do not like using fixed-spools, myself included, whilst others prefer them, but set-up correctly either will do the job so let's move onto looking at each type specifically.

FIXED SPOOLS

Advantages

1. Very easy to set-up.
2. Little maintenance or constant 'tuning' required.
3. Easy to cast with.
4. Adapts to adverse conditions very well.
5. Cheaper to buy than a multiplier.
6. Good rate of retrieve even with low-geared models.

Disadvantages

1. Distance suffers with lines above 0.4 mm diameter.
2. Rather heavy and clumsy to use.
3. Clutch has to be locked solid for hard casting.
4. Lack of 'feel' with hooked fish.
5. Twists line no matter how good the roller.
6. Care needed during hard casting to avoid bursting baits.

MULTIPLIERS

Advantages

1. Good 'feel' with hooked fish.
2. Good casting performance with a wide variety of line diameters.
3. Smoother clutch operation.
4. Light in weight and pleasant to use.
5. Gives the best results in terms of ultimate distance.
6. Better for reeling in heavy loads, i.e., fish & weed.

Disadvantages

1. Good models are expensive.
2. Requires constant 'tuning' for best results.
3. Difficult for beginners to control.
4. Requires constant maintenance to ensure long life.
5. Retrieve ratio can be too slow for snaggy ground with small models.

Fixed-spool Reels

Choosing

In this country fixed-spool reels have always been considered as rather second rate when it comes to surfcasting, yet abroad the opposite is true, the multiplier just doesn't get a look in. I can remember discussing the point with the then European sales manager for ABU who was desperately trying to promote the 6500 series and he told me that they just didn't want to know. The point was fully brought home when I fished a match in Belgium where apart from the English contingent who were all using multipliers there couldn't have been more than half a dozen other multipliers out of three hundred anglers.

Here though the fixed-spool user is always looked upon as a second class citizen and you can feel the kind of snobbery as the multiplier man tackles up next to his fixed-spool counterpart. Certainly multiplier users tend to feel that they already have an advantage and there is no doubt that after a long and often hard apprenticeship you get a feeling of satisfaction making long consistent casts with a multiplier. This is something that you never get with a fixed-spool and although I prefer a multiplier I would have no hesitation in changing if the fishing situation and conditions dictated that a fixed-spool would improve results.

For some tackle set-ups, notably back-casting, the fixed-spool is superior to the multiplier proving much easier to use when the reel is mounted at the bottom of the handle. In some fishing situations like match fishing for flatfish, pout or whiting where speed is paramount then a fixed-spool will have your tackle in and out again well ahead of the multiplier man. In this situation the time the bait is in the water is vital for success. On some venues there may be snags close inshore but clear ground well out and here a fixed-spool can be used to whip the lead in and speed it across the surface clear of the bottom. Try the same with a small multiplier and your arm will feel it's about to drop off. As you can see there are times when a fixed-spool is a definite advantage and therefore even a confirmed multiplier user would do well to keep one in his tackle bag.

So what are the points to look for? Well although you want as small and light a reel as is compatible with your fishing situation for distance casting you do need a fairly large spool. Large coils that come off the spool slowly are going to create less friction than small coils which will have to come off faster for the same amount of line and unfortunately large spools usually mean large heavy reels. The clutch mechanism also needs to be capable of locking the spool solid for hard casting so check for this, some models will not.

For years of reliable service a tough set of internal gears is a must and normally you get what you pay for in terms of quality. A cheap reel must be cheap for a reason and often that will be the type of metal used for, and the design of, the gears. This is not always the case but is often enough to warrant examination of the less expensive ones. Reels with rollers are better than those with full bail arms although these can be modified as you will see but check that the bail arm has a good roller where the line passes through.

As for models themselves most of the major manufacturers produce reasonable reels; Mitchell 498 and 486, D.A.M. Quick 5001, Sagarra Tarzan, Daiwa DF90, Penn 750 SS and the large Shakespeare models are all quite good. Beware though of very fast retrieves because although they whisk the line in quickly enough with just a sinker on they can be a real strain with a fish or weed on the end. Even quite low retrieve ratios are still much quicker than a lot of multipliers because of the much larger spool.

'Tuning'

The biggest 'killer' as far as distance casting with a fixed-spool is concerned is friction. There are two areas where this is a problem and they are (1) on the spool lip where the line rubs as it flows out, gradually increasing as the line level drops and (2) the rod rings, particularly the first one where the coils of line have to be compressed before they can pass through. In the section on rods you will see that for this type of reel only three large diameter intermediate rings are recommended plus a tip ring and these have been positioned as far away from the reel as practical. This will allow the coils to straighten slightly, thereby reducing diameter before they reach the first ring and then flow out through the others.

Moving on to the reel itself a little care and attention will ensure longer and smoother casts than would be the case if you just pulled it out of the box and wind on some line. Good design by the manufacturers could overcome most of these faults but they just don't seem to be bothered when it come to sea angling models. One or two are making an attempt and I was lucky enough to get one that Daiwa sell on their home market. It has a

Above—most fixed-spool reels lay line very poorly as standard.

Below—with correctly set-up backing the result is much better.

27

beautifully light body and spool with the spool being quite long and already shaped to 'cone' the line. Straight from the box the line lays on beautifully but unfortunately it just isn't quite large enough capacity-wise for our type of fishing.

Spool shape obviously varies from reel to reel but basically the front face needs to be of a slightly smaller diameter than the back so that the line can be built up to taper downwards from back to front. This is known as 'coneing' and will allow the line to flow off smoothly without the coils at the back having to drag their way across those at the front before getting clear. This is important for trouble free operation, because if one of those front coils is slightly loose it is sure to get dragged off by one of the rear ones before it should, causing a tangle. It is also better if the inside face of the front of the spool tapers slightly (see diagram). By sloping forwards, rather than being vertical as most are, the coils at the front of the spool can slip easily over the lip as the line level drops, rather than having to rise steeply producing extra drag. These may seem like small points and at short range they are relatively unimportant but with long casting the line leaves the spool at very high speed and then even small faults produce large effects.

So you want to look for a fairly large diameter, wide and well shaped spool but to make the best of it the reel's gearing mechanism needs to be arranged to lay the line on over the complete width in the previously mentioned 'cone' profile. Perfection would be the coils laid on in 'cotton-reel' fashion and the only reel I have ever seen that can do this is the Spanish Sagarra Tarzan (which proves it can be done). Unfortunately the spool on this particular reel is quite narrow and with the 0.4mm line I was using for tournaments at that

time the level dropped low far too quickly. Now with 0.35mm it should be much better. Even the reels that lay the line on fairly evenly (and there are many that do not) only fill part of the spool leaving gaps usually at the front or back.

The thing to do then with your spool, which will have a total capacity far greater than you will need, is to wind on some fairly thin string to reduce this capacity. The thing with string is that it is quite a soft material and even when packed down after a season's fishing it will still retain enough 'give' to absorb the crushing pressures of the line. Very thick monofilament isn't quite useless but will do at a push. Do not use thin monofilament line especially with light-weight plastic spools because it will eventually become packed harder and harder until finally the spool gets crushed. Arrange the backing to taper slightly from back to front, forming the basis of the 'cone' and fill the spool to approximately half way by hand winding.

Next start to wind on some line preferably a bit thicker than your fishing line, say about 20–25 lb BS using the reel itself and once it has covered the string look carefully at the way the bale arm is distributing the line. Odds on it will be up and down and probably all at the front or the back of the spool. To get it approximately in the middle of the spool you will need to take off the spool and either add a washer or two (to get the line nearer the back of the spool) or remove them (to get the line near the front). Some models such as the D.A.M. 5001 have a plastic washer under the spool with slots cut in it and these give a different variation in thickness by locating them on a steel peg. Therefore by simply taking off the spool all you need to do is turn the plastic washer to give the required position and pop it back on again.

EFFECT OF SPOOL SHAPE ON LINE FLOW

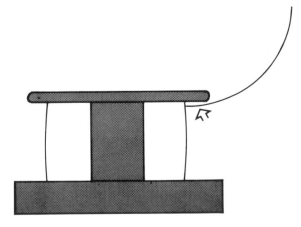

(A)
Inside face of front of spool is straight causing excessive friction as line level drops.

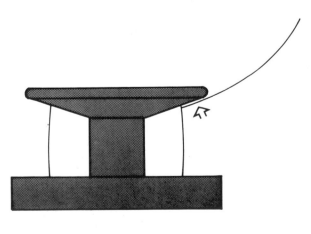

(B)
Inside face of front of spool is angled so that line still slips off smoothly as level drops.

'TUNING' A FIXED SPOOL

(A)
Fill the spool approximately half full with thin string or heavy mono so that it tapers down from back to front.

(B)
Wind on some backing-line that is slightly heavier than the fishing length using the bale-arm; it may end up looking like this.

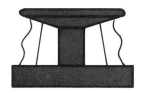

(C)
Strip off some of the backing-line and wind it on by hand so that it is opposite in shape to (B).

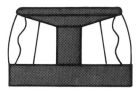

(D)
Finally top up with about 200 yds of fishing line. The backing should compensate for the gearing and should result in a level, slightly 'coned' spread of line.

To get rid of the humps and bumps you want to remove the spool and hand wind the line on in the opposite manner than the reel does it itself, taking care to maintain the 'cone' of course. This should be done to a level that will allow around 220–250 yards of actual fishing line to be placed on top and bring the level only very fractionally below the spool lip. Most of the tournament casters actually hump the line above the lips but they are after absolute maximum range and for fishing it would prove too much trouble to keep on the spool. On the field you can wind the line on with a tight, even pressure but on the beach this is often not possible; a full spool and loose line are the recipe for a tangle. Getting exactly the right amount of backing is of course luck at first but you soon learn how much your spool takes. Once it is done of course it is done for good for that breaking strain of line and by using a different colour you will know exactly how much to peel off when changing the fishing length (see diagrams).

Always use the thinnest diameter line that your fishing situation will allow because as I have said earlier line diameter affects distance potential with a fixed-spool considerably. Certainly line in the 0.3 – 0.35 mm (12–15 lb BS) will cope with virtually any snag free beach although you should always check it as you reel in for chafing. By holding it between thumb and forefinger you will keep the line under slight tension as it goes onto the spool and soon feel any chafing, or slight nicks. Thinner line cheats the tide better as well, helping the sinker to stay put during those hard running springs and also allowing sinker weight to be kept to a minimum for better sport.

Having put the line on correctly we can turn our attention to the reel itself. Some manufacturers have at last realised that a sea angler's fixed-spool does not really need a full bail arm and have therefore only fitted a roller. Bail arms are all right for the casual angler but once you get serious about casting they can be a nuisance, flying over in mid-cast with the inevitable results. One way of solving the problem is to fit a short length of elastic to the rod handle with a small hook on the other end. Then when you want to cast, you open the bail arm and place the hook on it. The tension of the elastic will stop it from inadvertently moving round and snapping over, a problem usually caused by the casting action making the handle rotate. The other way is to saw it off which is simpler and the only answer if your bail arm does not completely clear the spool as some do not. The roller end can be left, pulled out of the way for casting and then returned to its original position by simply turning the handle as usual. The line of course will have to be hooked round by hand but this is a small price to pay for a superior reel.

Another fault with fixed-spools is that the reel seat is too far away from the main body. This brings to light another problem and it is one that affects actual fishing rather than casting. It is usual to hold the line against the rod handle, or very close to it with the first finger and as it is released when casting there is a tendency to 'snatch'. I'm sure you've heard that 'twang' when someone casts with a fixed-spool and sometimes the noise is so loud it sounds more like the line parting. Normally at this stage the bait and hook go in separate directions especially softer ones like blow lugworm. The problem can be solved by using 'hook-ups' on the trace, a subject to be dealt with later and also by reducing the spool to handle distance. To do this take a two inch long piece of one inch O.D. dural and cut a slot about $\frac{1}{2}$ inch wide along its total length. Then straighten the edges in a vice to form a U-shape so that it will sit against the handle securely. It can then be held in place with insulating tape, reducing the gap considerably and therefore also reducing the line slap during casting.

Essentials for long range fishing with fixed-spools are the leather finger protector and the piece of dural tubing to reduce line snatch. Note the sawn-off bail arm to avoid mid-cast crack offs.

For a reel that is supposed to be simple to use there are quite a few points to sort out although many only begin to show up as you push your casting performances up. However, fixed-spools still remain easier to use, set-up and maintain than a multiplier, especially if you do not have the time or even want to master the techniques involved in multiplier use.

Multipliers

Choosing

Although fixed-spools hold a bigger percentage of the total reel sales for sea angling in this country there is no doubt that at the top end of the market, i.e. experienced anglers and casters, the multiplier is the number one choice. This is really due to two major reasons and they are that multipliers give that bit extra range over a wider range of line thickness, which also means fishing situations and that they are a lot smoother and more satisfying to use.

Of course tournament results have done much to promote the multiplier as the reel for distance and although these provide a useful guide it is actual fishing that matters. Many anglers have purchased a multiplier on such a recommendation only to be plagued with overruns and lost tackle. The inevitable result is to take it back to the tackle shop and swap it for a fixed-spool – which isn't giving the reel a chance. However, let me make it quite clear that no amount of braking will compensate for a bad, jerky casting style – unless you resort to Araldite in the bearings that is! A little careful 'tuning' can be done to help you out, slowing the spool enough to allow the novice to practice his casting technique without the fear that every cast is going to result in a crack-off.

It is also true that some models will never perform very well no matter how finely you 'tune' them because their design just will not allow it. Setting up the reel is a very important part of multiplier use but at least you want a reel that is designed well enough to give you a fighting chance. Confidence in your tackle is essential because nobody will be able to apply full power to a cast if he thinks something will go wrong especially during the learning stage. It is easier to iron out genuine casting problems when you know your reel is OK rather than having a niggling 'is it me or the reel?'. So how do you actually make your choice considering the vast range currently available and the type of fishing you will be doing? If you already do some fishing you will probably see more experienced anglers in action and close examination of the reels they prefer, plus of course a few probing questions will help no end. For anybody just starting this is more difficult but even so a wander along to one of your more popular local marks should give a clue together with a chat with an experienced, honest dealer.

What then are the points to consider for a casting/fishing multiplier? Well again you want to choose the smallest and lightest reel that suits your fishing situation best, particularly from a casting point of view because small lightweight multipliers are certainly the best. The spool particularly needs to be lightweight and fairly narrow, although it must still be very strong. Alloy is the best material for this job and the very best are machined from a single piece of metal. Spools which are pressed together tend to be forced apart after a while, gradually getting looser until they start running roughly because they are out of true or the end plates just buckle up. With this type it pays to remove the line after a hard session with heavy weed and rewind it under much less tension. A tape-recorder is ideal for this purpose. Plastic spools are also quite good but again they can break up if you are not careful and therefore the stripping and rewinding process is a must for long life.

Although the reel wants to be small it naturally must hold enough of the correct breaking strain line. For general beach work a capacity of 250 yards of 0.35 mm line is enough. That represents 12–15 lb BS and should handle any fairly snag free ground although some anglers use even lower breaking strains. With a multiplier though distance does not improve quite as dramatically as it does with a fixed-spool and I prefer to have some safety margin against wear and tear. If you do fish more mixed ground of course you will have to use thicker line anyway but pick the size of reel that accommodates it nicely and do not use big, heavy reels just for the sake of it; they are not needed.

Once the spool size gets too big or is made from a heavy material such as brass or steel the flywheel effect makes control very difficult indeed. At the moment of release a heavy spool is slow to start and then only accelerates slowly; conversely the light spools are very easy to start turning and accelerate fast maintaining the velocity of the sinker rather than dragging it down. The trouble gets worse as the heavy spool picks up speed, because the flywheel effect results in more line going off than the sinker requires; result – an overrun. Lightweight spools still have some flywheel effect of course but it is nowhere near as great and therefore the spool responds quickly as less line is required. Large heavy spools require so much braking to get them controllable that they will never be any good for distance work so steer well clear of them.

To get the best out of a small lightweight spool the cage needs to be robust enough to keep it running true and a total one piece frame is best. However the manufacturing costs are very high and some makes feature pressed together components which are usually very good when new but are easily distorted with abuse. Once the frame moves out of true you may have problems with the spool chafing on the side or running roughly because the bearings are not aligned. From this point of view the self-centreing bearings are better because although they can't allow for major damage, slight misalignments, due to knocks, can be accommodated. Self-centreing bearings have a rounded surface on the outer edge which allows them to move in the housing and therefore keep the spool running smoothly. With bearings that are fixed more securely a robust cage is a must.

The bearings themselves can be either phosphor bronze bushes or ball races. Personally I prefer ball races for smoothness and ease of lubrication but plain bushes are certainly very good. Although most tournament casters prefer the former the difference in distance is not enough to the angler. Plain bushes do tend to wear out more quickly and they also tend to wear the spool spindle considerably as well which is a bit of a nuisance when one considers the cost of a replacement spool. Furthermore, lubrication is less consistent with plain bushes because the oil tends to be pushed out from the bearing/spool spindle surfaces allowing the reel to run faster and faster until it is too free and overruns. You can take the end caps off every so often and re-oil but that is not a pleasant task on a cold, windy winter's night. Ball races on the other hand tend to hold the oil and prove more consistent over a longer period so out of the two they are worth the extra money.

Another feature of the more expensive reels is an inbuilt braking system. That is not to say that the cheaper reels are not worth using because they can be quite good but by far the most reliable and easy to use are those that have their own form of control. The most well known form of proper braking control (from this I am excluding end cap tension which is discussed in the following section on 'tuning') is the centrifugal system. With the centrifugal system a thin steel pin is fitted into the spool spindle parallel with the side faces of the spool. On the drive or check side of the reel, depending on which end the system is fitted there is a narrow drum and once the reel is assembled the steel pin runs inside this drum. The actual braking is done by small, cylindrical blocks which slide freely on the steel pin and as the spool spins the centrifugal force pushes them outwards until they meet and consequently rub on the inner surface of the drum. By varying the size and/or number of blocks the braking force can be varied; a surprisingly simple but very effective idea.

A newer system is one which involves magnetic forces to control the spool and up to the present time I have seen two different ones. The first is where a rare earth magnet is built into the check side housing and can be screwed in and out thereby moving it closer to or further away from the spool. Even though the spool is a non-magnetic alloy, currents are induced into it once it starts to spin and therefore it is attracted to the magnet. By varying the distance between spool and magnet the amount of drag is varied without the need to take the reel apart. The second system involves two banks of very small magnets mounted on the reel body and a steel drum mounted on the spool. The magnets are set in a circular pattern so that there is a small gap between them where the drum revolves. The magnets are arranged so that they alternate polarity; one acts as a north polarity and the next a south and so on. Also the outer magnets can be revolved by turning a dial on the drive side end plate; this dial is graduated so that you know how much braking is being applied and by moving the magnets so that the polarity of the outer and inner sets are either the same or opposite, the braking force is varied. For example when a north pole on the outer bank is aligned with a south pole on the inner the magnets attract and the currents acting on the drum slow down the spool. When a north pole on the outer bank is aligned with a north pole on the inner they repel each other and the spool spins freely. It may sound very technical but it is a very good set-up and for the angler the only concern is the graduated dial on the end to vary the braking force.

Again though there is no doubt that you get what you pay for in terms of reliability and long life. The cheaper reels can be quite good but need greater care in setting up for trouble free use. Most of the more expensive models certainly need care if they are to last but the braking systems make them much easier to set-up and use plus the ultimate distance potential is greater. For long range work on clean beaches where lines in the 0.35 – 0.40 mm (12–18 lb BS) are enough the small baitcasting multipliers have proved to be the most popular and effective. Reels such as the Daiwa 6HM, 6RM, ABU 6500 series and DAM 800B have proved themselves on the tournament court and beach although the Penn Squidder Junior, Surfmaster 100, Beachmaster 160 and Mitchell 602P make good alternatives if you cannot afford the former. If these are not robust enough or hold enough line of suitable breaking strain you may find the ABU 7000C, 8000 or even 9000 better along with the cheaper Penn Squidder, Surfmaster 150 or Mitchell 600P. But be warned, once you step up in reel size, distance will suffer and therefore you must take into account your fishing situation and decide on how large a part casting will play.

'Tuning'

'Tuning' a multiplier is all about one thing and that is to get it casting smoothly without overruns. For

Above—the well tried and tested centrifugal braking system. Braking force is varied by the size and number of blocks.

Below—the more modern Daiwa magnetic braking system. Although it looks complicated its use is very straight-forward.

most anglers starting off this is the number one problem and although there is virtually no cure against jerky casting there are ways of slowing the spool down to allow a beginner to learn to cast, then gradually speeding it up as he gets better.

The reason that a multiplier overruns is because the spool feeds more line than the flying sinker can drag away with it. Therefore the excess winds back on itself and subsequently tangles, so the idea must be to get the two to balance. Ideally the spool should feed exactly the right amount of line to the sinker resulting in as little drag as possible but in practice this hardly ever works. Even an expert caster cannot guarantee perfection every time and the weather is very rarely perfect; a slip of the foot or a gust of wind would be enough to create trouble. Therefore it pays to set-up the reel with a small safety margin to allow for any problems especially for practical fishing because lost line and tackle spoil any session.

From a control viewpoint it is better to consider reels with and without braking controls separately.

(1) Without braking controls Under this heading comes most of the cheaper range multipliers such as the Mitchell 602 series and many of the Penn reels. To get them to cast smoothly requires both a smooth casting style and considerable care in setting the reel up otherwise they can be difficult to use. Often unfortunately, beginners go for these reels because of their low price not realising that they need some knowledge of reels to sort them out and inevitably they fail, possibly to the extent of being put off multipliers for good.

To say there is no braking control is not strictly true because there is usually a screwed end cap on one of the side plates which can be wound in to bring pressure onto the spool spindle. This is really a last resort method because bearing and spindle wear is greatly increased and there is a tremendous loss in distance. With the reel assembled the cap should be screwed down until there is just a hint of side play in the spool and that is where it should stay, and then attention should be paid to lubrication and line level. These are the two factors that will govern the way the reel ultimately performs and each is inter-related. Let us look at each in turn.

Firstly, line level. This is very important because just as a heavy metal spool gives trouble so can loading the reel with too much line. The reason is the same, too much line will make the spool heavy and give it a flywheel effect during the cast. Therefore you want to have enough so that the line level is not ridiculously low after the cast has been made but not too much so that it causes problems. You should find that a final line level of approximately three quarters of the total capacity about right; once you exceed that the reel will be hard to control. Even the smaller Penns, etc hold well in excess of 200 yards of 0.35 mm line and even

0.40 mm, so you need to put some backing on first. Thin string, dacron or some other fairly soft material is good. As with fixed-spool reels some trial and error may be needed to get the final level correct but once you have it right it is done for good.

Next is lubrication. Most of the cheaper reels have plain bush bearings although a few do have ball bearings, but the thickness of the oil you use to lubricate them will have a pronounced effect on the way the spool runs whichever type is fitted. The thinner the oil the faster the spool will run and therefore you want to find the one that lets the reel cast well with your technique. For most reels without other forms of braking than end cap tension very thin oils such as 3 in 1 are usually too thin even for experienced casters. Usually a general purpose 20/50 motor oil is about as thin as you want and therefore a beginner should be looking at something around SAE90 or even SAE 140 grade to begin with. Naturally temperature is likely to affect the oil quite a bit; oil that is just right on a cold winter's day may be too thin in the summer so you may find it necessary to use a slightly different grade at each time of year. Also with plain bush reels the oil is forced out of the bearings quicker than it is with ball races so you may need to add a couple of drops of oil at certain times during a long session.

This may all seem like a lot of trouble to go to and I suppose it is but unfortunately it is the only way to have a reel that behaves. Anyway once you have the line level and oil grades that suit you best then it is easy to keep the reel running sweetly but it is getting to that stage that is hardest. You may find that different grades of oil have a greater effect than you wish; one grade is too thin, the next too thick and here you can either mix the two to get it just right or add a little more line to the spool. This will cause the reel to run that bit faster as well and therefore by adding or removing 10–20 yards of line you can get it just right. Remember of course to adjust the backing level next time you change your line to give the correct level with a full 200 yards of fishing line on top.

(2) With braking controls These reels are much easier to set-up and use particularly for the beginner because even with thin oil and a bit too much line on the spool the braking system can be set to compensate. However, for the very best performance it still pays to get everything right because no reel is absolutely foolproof.

Let us start off, then, with line level. This is not quite so critical as it was with the cheaper reels but it is still possible to overfill them to the level where severe braking is needed to keep them in order. The small baitcasters hold two hundred yards of 0.40 mm (15–18 lb BS) line comfortably although it is possible to squeeze on 260 yards if you lay it on very carefully. However the spool would be 'humped' in the middle to get that amount on and for fishing purposes this is far too much. With 0.35 mm (12–15 lb BS) you can put a little backing on the spool before the fishing length of about 200 yards to form a cushion although the finished level needs to be kept to about 1/16 inch below the spool lips. The larger models are usually only necessary if you particularly need a lot of line in reserve perhaps when fishing for shore tope, or for lines in excess of 0.45 mm which is unusual on distance marks. However, the line level can be set between about ¾ to ⅞ full, with an appropriate amount of backing beneath the fishing length of course, which is higher than the Penns, etc because the braking system will compensate for this easily.

Lubrication is easy also because a nice medium grade oil such as 20/50 or straight 30 will be ideal. It is thin enough to allow smooth, free running for good distances but has enough 'body' to give some degree of control by itself. However if you do find that the two extremes of the controlling system are not what you want such as when the brake is completely off the spool it still does not run freely enough or when completely 'on' it is too free, then you can use a thicker or thinner oil to get exactly what you want. Even reels of the same make and design run differently but you should find that variations can be compensated by the braking

system rather than going to the trouble of changing oil grade. I also put a small drop of oil on the spool spindle where it runs through the drive gear which also seems to add a small amount of braking. Sometimes the line just starts to lift and all that is needed is a drop of oil placed there to smooth it out rather than having to increase the braking control.

However, with the line level and lubrication settled the real control comes with either the centrifugal system or the magnetic system whichever type you prefer. The way that these systems work has already been explained so I will move on straight away to how they are adjusted. The newer magnetic control is very straightforward indeed being varied simply by turning the adjuster on the end plate of the reel. Gradually set it lower until you find the setting where your reel runs smoothly with no line lift at all although you may feel that a setting higher or lower can be used with strong tail or headwinds. As all adjustment is external there shouldn't be any difficulties. With the centrifugal system the braking is varied by the size and number of blocks used. By all means start with the largest size which would prove enough even for learning to cast from scratch. Then as you improve you can reduce the size to medium, then small and finally one small or even none at all. Using only one does not upset the balance of the spool. It is easy to remove the spool and slip on another block when

Cheaper reels such as this Penn Surfmaster 150 Junior are still capable of giving a very good fishing/casting performance when set-up correctly.

fishing into a headwind or using very large baits. Large chunks of herring can upset even the smoothest cast.

Whatever type of multiplier you finally purchase the key is to slow it down enough to cope with your own standard of casting. On the field either in practice or on the tournament court you can afford to run your reel a little bit on the fast side so that say, you get four out of five casts away because of the need for absolute distance. However for practical fishing this is pretty useless because condi-tions are rarely perfect and a baited trace makes the sinker slow down much quicker than it does by itself. Therefore you always want to set the reel slightly on the slow side to allow for a slip of the foot or puff of wind. Confidence in the reel will mean that you will cast that bit harder anyway probably making up the distance as well, and of course you won't lose tackle and will enjoy your fishing that much more. To give you some start-ing point I have drawn up a chart which should help.

'Tuning' a Multiplier

Reel Type	Line Level	Lubricant	Brake Setting	Casting Conditions
No built-in braking system, plain bush bearings & medium capacity spool e.g.: Penn 100, 160 Mitchell 602 AP, etc.	$\frac{3}{4}$ full	SAE 140	—	Beginners
		SAE 90	—	Average caster. Suitable for most conditions with average size baits
		SAE 20/50	—	Good casters. Maximum range in favourable conditions.
Centrifugal brakes, ball bearings, small spool e.g.: ABU 6500, Daiwa 6HM D.A.M. 800 B, etc.	Just below spool lips	SAE 20/50	2 large blocks	Beginners
			2 small blocks	Average caster – most conditions & bait sizes
			1 small block	Good caster – most conditions & average size baits
			—	Tournament casting
Centrifugal brake, bush bearings, medium capacity spool. e.g.: ABU 7000, Daiwa Procaster PS 57.	$\frac{3}{4} - \frac{7}{8}$ full	SAE 20/50	4 small or 2 large blocks	Beginners
			2 small blocks	Average caster – most conditions, average size baits
			1 small block	Good casters – most conditions, average size baits
Magnetic brake, any design. e.g.: Daiwa Magforce, PMF 55 & 57 H, Penn Magpower 970, ABU Mag II & Ultra Mag II.	Just below spool lips	SAE 10/20 or 3 in 1 thick	$\frac{3}{4}$ – max dial setting.	Beginners
			$\frac{1}{4} - \frac{3}{4}$ dial setting.	Average caster – most conditions & bait size
			$0 - \frac{1}{4}$ dial setting	Good caster – most conditions & bait size

Line

It is not so many years ago that the average strength of main line used by shore anglers, even over clean ground was in excess of 20 lb. I can remember using only 18 lb and considering myself quite a dare-devil, although of course I still used a casting leader of 30 lb which by today's standards is very light. Anglers then however had less need to cast the distances that today's shore man must because fish were generally much more numerous and therefore easy to catch. Unfortunately the picture now is not quite as rosy and tackle and casting styles have had to be considerably improved in the quest for better bags of fish. As a result of this, lines have come under scrutiny as well and now most anglers use quite thin main lines of 0.33 mm (12 lb BS) to 0.40 mm (18 lb BS) along with very strong leaders in the 0.65 mm (45 lb BS) to 0.8 mm (60 lb BS) range.

Main line You would think that due to the very nature of the sea shore heavy swells, sand and shingle rasping away at the line and because of the distance involved between angler and fish you should use a very strong line. This is not the case however because modern nylon lines resist these elements much better than you would imagine and also the amount of pressure that you can actually exert with a conventional rod and reel is surprisingly low. Set up your tackle and run out, say, 100 yards of line which will probably be less than you will have out in a practical angling situation. Get a friend to tie the end of your line to a spring balance and then note the readings as you pull the rod up to apply the pressure. Even if you are very strong and your rod powerful you would do very well indeed to see a greater reading than about 9 lb and this only for a very short period of time while you pulled at your very hardest. The leverage against you is so great that you just cannot maintain it for any length of time and also the natural stretch in monofilament line will absorb some of your effort. You can see therefore from this experiment that standard fishing tackle cannot exploit the performance of lines over 10 lb BS anyway.

However the nature of the sea-shore is abrasive and it would be foolish not to allow some margin for safety. A slight cut from a small stone would reduce such a thin line as 10 lb BS very quickly indeed to a level that would not be tolerable. Thin nylon has a relatively large surface area for its strength and therefore once damaged its breaking strain rapidly reduces. As you increase the breaking strain however the surface area increases re-latively slowly and therefore abrasion resistance is much better. Obviously you reach a point where the line is just too thick and fishing performance falls off so a happy medium has to be reached. So to allow for some wear and tear you should find that snag free venues are adequately covered by a main line of about 15 lb BS (0.35 – 0.40 mm) which should give the best compromise between strength and diameter for both casting and fishing. Should you become snagged you will find that with un-damaged line the only way to break-off is to point the rod directly at the obstruction and steadily walk back. A tip here is to try pulling from a position both up and down tide of your fishing position until the line is just below breaking point; sometimes the different angle is enough to free the tackle.

If this does not work I then pull directly up the beach until the line is virtually breaking and then hold it there for a few seconds. This steady, heavy pressure will sometimes pull an obstruction like old tackle out of the sand or a sinker through clay whereas sudden pressure would only have broken the line.

Having decided to use a line of about 15 lb BS you can now look more closely into the various makes of line available. The first thing that will strike you if you pick up a few different brands is that they are not all the same diameter. Most will fall into the 0.35 – 0.40 mm range already mentioned but a few will be thicker and a few thinner. Really anything over 0.40 mm should be discounted because once you exceed this, casting distance will suffer. Also the water pressure in strong tidal areas could be excessive, creating the need for heavy sinkers, i.e. in excess of 6 oz. 0.35 mm seems to be average and most 15 lb lines of this diameter represent a good middle-of-the-road choice in terms of quality and price.

Brands like Sylcast, Gantel, Milbro, Triple Fish and DAM Strike are the right thickness, fairly resistant to abrasion, fairly soft and stretchy enough to be easy to handle. Being available in bulk spools, which is the only way to buy your line, the price is not prohibitive. Of course there are thinner lines available which are still rated at 15 lb BS and some even higher but these are usually very expensive or pre-stretched lines or both. When you are learning to cast, highly priced line is obviously out because you will probably use a hell of a lot! Even when you have mastered casting to a reasonable level, mistakes still happen and the extra distance really is not worth the money. Also if the line is pre-stretched it tends to be rather brittle compared to the cheaper 'premium' lines and I have found that their resistance to the general rigours of beach angling is not very good. If you do want to use thinner line then go for a lower breaking strain such as 12 lb BS and just make sure that you only use it for a couple of sessions, reverse it to use the other end for another couple then throw it away. Line this thin however will obviously have a reduced safety margin and although quite a few anglers on my local East Anglian coastline use line this thin I prefer to stick with the 15 lb BS/0.35 mm combination. Also if you do buy in bulk keep the spool in a cool dark place so that it will last well because direct sunlight is supposed to weaken the line to some degree.

Leaders Some of the reason that anglers once used lines of 20 lb BS plus was that they needed the strength to take the pressure of casting. Today's techniques would snap these like cotton and conversly there is no way that 50 lb BS all-through is going to cast well. A leader is basically a short length of very strong line tied to the end of the main reel line and it is there mainly to absorb the stresses of casting. This is a job that it must carry out successfully cast after cast throughout the session even though the stones and sand have been doing their best to wear it away. Also it can offer some insurance against losing a big fish when you get into the breakers when the undertow is doing its best to drag it off the hook. At this point the last thing you need is suspect line although the length of the leader and the amount of weed about at the time will have a great deal of bearing on how effective it really is.

So the leader is there to act as a shock absorber when casting and although in theory a perfectly smooth cast, where the lead is following the rod tip's path, puts very little strain on the line in practice this state of affairs is rare and the line experiences quite a considerable strain. Therefore the strong length of nylon gives you the confidence to really hit the rod hard knowing that the line will not break; a point that is vitally important on a crowded beach or harbour wall. Today's caster needs to be particularly safety conscious because a crack-off in mid-cast on a crowded venue can spell disaster to a neighbour. That in itself makes the use of a leader a moral obligation and luckily most anglers appreciate this, although there are still some idiots who do not. Even when you are using a leader however, check it regularly for small cuts or other signs of abrasion which will reduce its strength and render it virtually useless.

The use of the leader then allows you to use much lighter and consequently thinner line, which by itself would not stand a chance of holding a powerful cast. Therefore even with very heavy sinkers of 6 oz upwards you can still use standard 15 lb BS/0.35 mm running line over clean ground which brings benefits as far as the reel is concerned. Enough line can be stored on small lightweight multipliers which are better for casting, much better balanced and generally nicer to use than models which accommodate around 200 yards of 35 lb BS line. Fixed-spools perform much better with the thinner line and of course on the beach the smaller surface area helps cheat the tide keeping your terminal tackle in place with relatively lightweight sinkers.

From a casting aspect the leader needs to be long enough so that with terminal tackle clipped on the end and the drop length set there are still at least five complete turns around the reel spool. Any less than this with a multiplier could prove particularly hazardous because due to the wet line the spool can slip slightly beneath the thumb during casting and you need to allow for this. By using only a couple of turns all the strain will be transferred to the light line with the inevitable result. Also the leader needs to be short enough so that it has cleared the rod rings before the sinker has reached its maximum velocity. Otherwise it has a tendency to catch one of the rings and get broken or even rip the ring away from its whipping, so very long leaders are also out.

Therefore with a limited length of leader you are limited to how near you can actually get to the waves. On shallow beaches the wash can come rushing up the beach with enough force to soak you even with thigh boots on. Therefore there is no way that you are going to get the leader onto the spool before the fish is actually through the waves. Also there is nearly always some floating weed about which will cling to the main line and gradually work down to the knot where the leader is joined. As soon as this reaches the tip ring it will jam and although using a reasonable sized ring helps slightly it's not the complete answer so again the leader will never reach the ring. The only answer in these circumstances is to take care and learn to land your fish properly – a subject dealt with under *Fishing Techniques*.

The exact strength of the leader will depend on the sinker weight. For weights of 5 oz or more the leader needs to be very strong, at least 45 lb BS and line of this thickness (perhaps 0.8 mm) can be rather stiff and springy. The hard lines such as Bayer and Sylcast are very strong indeed and these are my choice for punishing duties such as field practising and tournaments, but on the beach I tend to opt for something slightly softer such as Gantel. Although in the lower breaking strains you can't notice too much difference, in the higher strengths there is quite a difference and I prefer the softer line particularly for terminal tackle. However, as long as the breaking strain is high enough (see table) it shouldn't matter which make you actually buy, but once you have tried a few I am sure you will find one that is preferred.

The way the leader is positioned on the spool can make a difference as well. With a fixed-spool the bail arm will lay it on for you and the exact position of the knot is relatively unimportant for fishing but for casting competitions I hand wind the leader on and place the knot on the back edge of the spool. It can then fly off cleanly rather than having other coils of leader dragged over it, as would happen if it was placed further forward. This reduces the chance of loose coils being pulled away causing a 'bunch'. With a multiplier the leader knot wants to be positioned on one side of the spool and so really does all the leader turns. This is so that there is no risk of the leader knot cutting your thumb if the spool slips and also so that the thumb lays on the nice level area of thin line thereby increasing grip.

A few turns of heavy line distributed across the spool make it rather lumpy and more difficult to hold. The strain of casting is also taken as near the supporting bearing as possible rather than in the centre where it could flex the spindle slightly.

Sinker Weight	Leader Strength (Minimum)
3 oz	28 lb
4 oz	35 lb
5 oz	45 lb
6 oz	50 lb
7 oz	55 lb
8 oz	60 lb

Knots

The breaking strain of a line quoted on the label of the spool is a guide to what it should stand up to dry. Once waterlogged the breaking strain will be reduced slightly and once you tie a knot in it the breaking strain will be reduced considerably, especially of it is not tied properly. The lighter main line should have only one knot in it if possible and that will be where it joins the leader. This should be the weakest part of the link between the reel and the hook and if you are unlucky enough to get snagged, as we do sooner or later, this is where the line will part. You have lost the leader and trace but at least the main line is intact which it possibly would not be if you had other knots along its length.

Most of the knots will be on the trace, joining line to links or swivels, line to hooks and other stop knots or stand-off knots. These are the ones that will be taking the strain of hard casting and although they will be tied with a heavy breaking strain they will soon give way if they are not tied properly. It is probably fair to say that there is as much tackle lost because of bad knots as there is through bad casting; on a crowded beach the danger aspect cannot be over-emphasised. In fact for traces I usually use line that it is a bit heavier than the leader itself; about 5 lb BS increase usually allows for loss due to knotting so, if I was using a 50 lb BS leader then my traces would be made of 55 lb BS line.

There must be hundreds of different types of knots and I have been shown all sorts, some quite simple to tie and others very difficult. Very complicated knots such as the Bimini Hitch are a waste of time unless you are into line class records when with very light lines you cannot afford to lose breaking strain at all. Basically I use only four knots for fishing and all of these are based on the blood knot. They are easily tied, reliable and have a strength of about 90% of the original line which should be good enough for general beach work. The knot needs to be simple because you may need to repeat it on a bitterly cold winter's night, when your fingers are frozen to the bone.

Firstly then we'll look at the half blood knot. This is a very tough and easily tied knot which forms a basis for many others. It is used to secure hooks, swivels, split rings etc, although make sure that you never tie directly onto the sinker. If you do, the knot and line being rigidly attached gets cut and chafed far worse than it does if you connect via a swivel or split ring. The flexible nature of an additional link protects the line considerably. To tie the knot push the end of the line through the eye of the swivel and then turn it back on itself winding it around for at least six turns. Finally, push the end through the loop between the swivel eye and the first turn, moisten with saliva then gradually pull up tight. I usually pull the loose end as well to tighten up the coils. A slight modification and an improvement in some people's opinion is to give the knot a final tuck (see diagram) although I find the standard knot, properly tied, adequate.

Next is the standard blood knot which as its name suggests is two half blood knots together. It is used to join two lines of approximately the same diameter although some anglers still use it for joining the running line to the leader where it really is not suitable. To tie the knot hold the two lines together but facing in opposite directions and wind one around the other four to five times. Take the free end back to the start of the turns and push it between the two lines. Next wind the other line around again four to five times then take it back to the start so that it goes through the same gap as the first line but in the opposite direction. Wet the line and pull up gradually.

Thirdly we have the stand off knot or blood loop. This knot is used on a paternoster rig to hold the hook snoods and does away with the need for metal booms. To tie the knot form a loop in the line with the free ends held together and pointing in opposite directions. Holding the lines where they are together, turn them either clockwise or anti-clockwise, it doesn't really matter, putting twists into the two lines in both directions from the central holding position, about six to seven turns. The loop is then pushed through the gap between the two lines in the centre, wetted and gradually pulled up. If you want a short, stiff boom you can put some twists into the loop before tying the knot or tie a large loop, twist it, then pour some boiling water over it. Cool it off under the cold tap and you will find that the twists stay put. Only a small modification but one that certainly is an improvement.

Finally we have the leader knot for joining two lines of greatly differing diameters. Joining the leader to the running line demands a smooth knot to avoid the chance of it catching a ring and causing a crack-off. With the standard blood knot it is virtually impossible to get the turns of heavy nylon to tighten up with the lighter more flexible main line. The resulting knot also tends to be bulky which as mentioned is not to be recommended. The leader knot is formed by firstly tying a simple overhand knot in the thick line, but do not pull it up tight. Pass the thin line through the front of the overhand knot then pull it tight. Wind the thin line around the thick line forming six to seven turns, take the thin line back to the start and push it between the thick and thin lines next to the over-hand knot making two turns around the thick line. Moisten and gradually pull up. A neater smaller knot can be made by flattening the end of the thick line forming a small 'spade-end' and then piercing it with a needle or hook point. The thin line is then passed through the hole doing away with the need for an overhand knot. Tournament casters use this knot to reduce the chance of it catching to a minimum, but for practical fishing I would stick with the standard knot.

You will notice that with all the knots I have said 'moisten and gradually pull up'. Monofilament line tends to be 'sticky' when you try to pull up knots and moistening with saliva helps the turns to slide down the line allowing the knot to be pulled up really tightly. This is also the reason for pulling up gradually because if you give the line a sudden jerk the turns will tighten onto the line before the knot is fully pulled up or even burn the line reducing its breaking strain. Always check that the knot has fully tightened and then trim off any surplus with snips leaving a tail of about $\frac{1}{8}$ inch in case of any slight slipping.

Sinkers

Apart from a few specialised situations such as spinning or float-fishing most beach fishing is carried out with the bait anchored on the sea bed. Due to the very nature of the sea this often requires the use of a substantial weight usually more than three ounces and sometimes as much as eight. Even on days when the sea is calm and there is little wind or tide you often need to use at least five ounces to carry your bait out to the fish and unfortunately the use of a heavy sinker is often a must.

This does not mean that just any old chunk of lead will do because in many situations the weight and design of the sinker will make quite a difference to how the bait is presented. However, from the many sets of lost tackle I have retrieved over the years quite a fair proportion of beach anglers are not too bothered about either point. Certainly there are times when the only priority is that the bait is on the bottom, so as long as the sinker is capable of doing this it is good enough and over really rough weedy ground I would not hesitate to use a makeshift sinker. At other times though the fish can be fussy and by selecting the right sinker you can manage to pull out a few whilst other anglers remain fishless.

For general beach work the weight and shape of your sinker should be decided upon after considering the circumstances that govern your particular fishing situation; bait type and size, sea conditions, weather conditions, casting distance, species of fish and even casting style and your own physique. That's quite a list and obviously it becomes quite easy to decide once you have fished an area for a few years. Then experience takes over but for the newcomer it pays to have a basic understanding of the different designs and how they behave. Armed with this knowledge you can at least make a reasonable choice.

THE SINKERS FUNCTION

Basically a sinker has to carry out two functions:

(1) It has to take the terminal tackle and bait to the required position.
(2) Once it has reached that position it has to take the terminal tackle and bait to the sea bed and either anchor it there or allow it to move in a controlled manner to aid presentation.

Really these are very simple functions in themselves but once you also take into account the wide range of conditions that the beach angler has to face they become rather more complex. The problem is that you need to have a range of sinkers in your tackle box that will allow good casting and fishing throughout the full range of fishing conditions because no one design is likely to offer all the solutions. However, carrying them all down to the beach would be a different matter, more suited to Geoff Capes! In practice you can usually make a good guess at the types you will need which will keep the number required down to a reasonable amount.

The first of the two functions concerns the casting potential of the sinker. The idea behind a developed, powerful casting technique is to transfer power from your body into the sinker thereby accelerating it to high speed so that it becomes a massive propulsive force, hurtling out to sea. This power will gradually be expended as the sinker tows the terminal tackle and bait out to the required position, which is its task. To do this it has to overcome air drag, gravity and the mechanised friction of line and reel and the further you need to cast the greater these resisting factors become.

Most anglers who have mastered a good casting technique can put a plain weight in the 2–8 oz range far enough for most fishing circumstances. However you will find that the very best distances come within a band much narrower than that, probably as narrow as $\frac{1}{2}$ oz. Exactly which weight it turns out to be depends largely on your casting style, rod length and physique but for most averagely built people it usually falls within the $4\frac{1}{2}$–6 oz range. I find that my best distances are obtained with a sinker in the 5–$5\frac{1}{2}$ oz bracket but you may do better with slightly more or less depending on the factors mentioned.

It is the 'momentum' or carrying ability of the sinker that holds the key to the distance cast and as any mechanics students will tell you momentum = mass × speed. From this it is immediately apparent that an eight ounce sinker has only to fly at half the speed of a four ounce sinker to generate the same momentum. That is just as well because you would be a very powerful person if you could cast an eight ounce sinker as fast as a four ounce! The trouble comes however with sinkers that need to travel at high speed because problems arise with casting, bait presentation and reel control.

You may find that over grass with the wind behind you that a $4\frac{1}{2}$ oz sinker travels furthest but under fishing conditions things are not quite the same. Attach a baited trace and immediately the drag is increased particularly in the head winds which seem to be the norm when I go fishing. High sinker speeds compound the effects of drag which is one of the reasons that it seems to require a super human effort to reach 200 yds even though you can consistently reach 195–197 yds. The lighter sinker therefore is affected far more than the 6 oz sinker which will be travelling that much more slowly for the same momentum.

With lighter sinkers the casting action has to be that much quicker. Again on the field this may not be too much of a problem but on the beach where your footing is likely to move in the soft sand or the beach rises steeply behind you it can create problems. A slight mistake and casting distance will drop considerably and problems can occur with the reel, particularly multipliers. The high initial velocity of the sinker makes reel control very difficult; it has to be free enough to maintain this speed at the start of the cast but retain enough drag to control the spool as the sinker rapidly slows towards the end. It is a combination that is very difficult to achieve even for experienced tournament casters, let alone the average angler.

Baits also suffer under high accelerating forces particularly soft ones like blow lugworm which will literally disintigrate due to wind pressure. Even some of the tougher ones will be badly torn and look extremely second rate when they arrive on the sea bed. Again the heavier, slower travelling sinker has the advantage but eventually you will come to the stage where physically it becomes very difficult to handle any more weight, apart from spoiling the fight from fish. Therefore the optimum weight will be found and you may find that this is a bit heavier than your optimum on the field. $4\frac{1}{2}$ oz may go 200 yds in the field but take a bait only 140 yds on the beach dropping to 110 yds in bad weather. $5\frac{1}{2}$ oz may only go 190 yds on the field but manage 150 yds with bait and still 125 yds in bad weather.

Ideally from the sport point of view the weight of the sinker should be kept to a minimum, particularly when one considers that the majority of shore caught fish weigh 5 pounds or less. If I could use 2 oz sinkers then I would but as we have seen in practice this is not really a realistic proposition. For long range fishing 5 oz is a realistic minimum to reach the required position and for the second function, to hold it there. Although the sea may calm with the wind coming off the land the pressure of the tide acting on the running line will just sweep anything less away. More often than not even a plain 5 oz sinker will not hold steady in anything above a gentle flow. Rather than increase the weight above that which you feel is the most comfortable to use attention has to be paid to the shape of the sinker and/or the use of anchor wires. By doing this the holding properties of the sinker are greatly improved (and so are the fishing properties); really it is a case of finding the optimum combination of design and weight for both pleasurable and effective angling.

SINKER DESIGN

The most popular design of sinker at the moment is the casting bomb. The basic bomb shape including all the slight variations has excellent aerodynamic properties with no single design having a particular advantage. Invariably any of them cast well and problems will only arise if the body is too long because this will cause the sinker to 'tumble' in flight. Users of fixed-spool reels will find that this is a problem more than multiplier users, because of the method of releasing the line with the former.

A plain bomb has very little in the way of gripping properties by itself and therefore over rough ground you have a reasonable chance of getting your terminal tackle back. Mind you if it is really that bad old spark plugs, nuts and bolts and cycle inner tubes filled with sand are a better bet because you will have to pull for a break on most casts. Strong lateral tides will soon sweep even a heavy bomb ashore which is absolutely useless but at certain times when the tide has virtually stopped, a bomb can sometimes be used with success.

When the tide is really moving though the fish tend to feed better and then the problem of holding out increases. Therefore to avoid the use of a ridiculous amount of lead a bomb shaped sinker can be equipped with wires protruding from the nose or the sides. The wires are bent out like an anchor to dig into the bottom but the problem then arises of reeling in. Even over a clear sandy bottom retrieving can be difficult but almost impossible on soft mud or where it's a bit weedy, and any fish hooked are not likely to put up much of a struggle. The answer is to use wires which will swing back

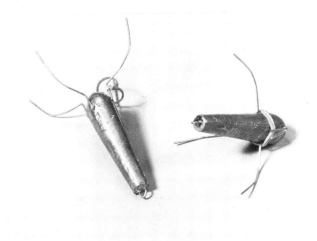

Breakaway sinkers in the 'grip' and 'broken-out' positions. This design has done much to encourage lighter tackle for sea fishing.

on the retrieve as on the patented Breakaway sinkers.

This is an idea that stands out as being obvious but beach anglers struggled for many years before the design was invented. The sinker is the standard bomb shape with four channels in the side situated at 90° to each other. The wires are pushed through small holes located just behind the nose and bent up to align with the channels. A bead is slid onto each wire and it is these beads which hold the wires in the anchoring position and therefore gripping the bottom. Extra pressure is applied by drawing the rod back when you want to reel in, the beads are pulled out of the channels, the wires swing back and you can easily reel in. Because the idea is patented you are not allowed to produce the same type for re-sale but you can make your own and I do so using an elastic band to hold the wires in position rather than beads. By trial and error you soon find the best length of wires and band tension to hold out in the tide yet easily 'break-out' when you want to wind in.

By using fairly long wires I find that even a $5\frac{1}{2}$ oz bomb will hold out in really bad conditions but if tidal flow really is excessive there are two things you can do. One is to clip one of the plastic Breakaways above your standard weight which then adds very little in the way of extra weight but a lot in gripping ability. Secondly is to use a slightly heavier fixed wire sinker and the type to go for are those with wires protruding from the nose. Under really heavy pressure or if they get hooked up on a rock the wires will spring back enough to release it particularly if you use a fairly soft flexible wire. This can be very important if you fish some of the very popular venues which tend to become a mass of lost lines by early winter and reeling in is like trying to get your terminal tackle through a barbed wire fence. The fixed wire sinkers to avoid are those where the wires emerge from the side because unless you use a very soft wire they are hard to reel in and hook-up on anything in their path. The narrow angle between lead and wire is a certain trap for lost lines so keep well clear of this design or expect to lose a lot of tackle.

Wired bombs handle most fishing situations but there are other designs around although many are localised in their use and some limited in effectiveness. In my area the pyramid design was once very popular but is not often seen now. It doesn't have any wires but relies purely on its pyramid shape to help it grip the bottom, a job that it performs fairly effectively over soft ground like sand or mud by ploughing in. The loop for line attattchment is fitted in the centre of its square base and therefore it still casts quite well but obviously because its frontal

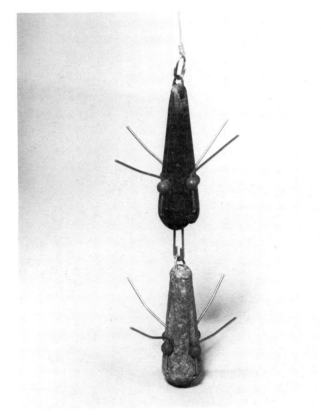

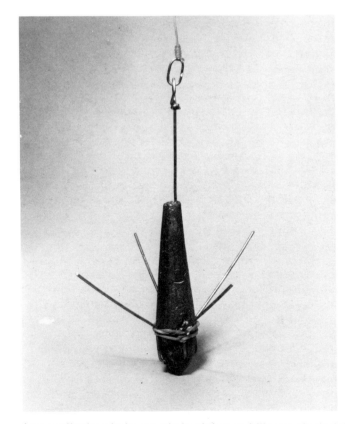

Extra grip without extra weight is offered by using one of the plastic Breakaway sinkers above the more conventional one.

Long tail wires help greatly in sinker stability particularly for fixed-spool casters. Extra grip is also claimed for this design.

area is much greater than a bomb it is second best as far as distance is concerned. Pyramid sinkers do not grip as well as wired sinkers but it is still enough to jerk the trace and sink the hook in when a fish moves off with the bait. They are also reasonably easy to retrieve although they do tend to 'stick' slightly as they tumble over the bottom, a tendency that I find particularly annoying with a fish on.

Grip or 'watch' leads, which resemble a large polo mint with lumps on, are common on hand-lines and that is where they should stay being of very limited use for anything else. Star leads which look like the thing medieval knights swing around on the end of a chain cast about as well as a brick, do not hold the bottom and as such only deserve to be melted down and made into something more useful and that goes for many other shapes and sizes. Some of the spoon patterns are quite good over very rough ground because they don't fall into cracks easily and plane up from the bottom quite well if you wind in quickly. They are not exactly aerodynamic but cast far enough for use on the ground they are meant for because absolute distance is rarely necessary.

Before leaving the subject of sinker design I must mention a very interesting device called the Baitsafe. The Baitsafe is basically a sinker but has a plastic bait carrying capsule as an integral part of it. The lead forming the weight is in the nose part along with the wires and these carry out the tack of anchoring the tackle to the bottom. Behind this the plastic part is shaped rather like a coffin with a detachable lid allowing access to put the baited hook inside. The lid is then put back on by locating a wedge shaped piece of plastic at the end of the lid into a slot in the lead, thereby keeping the bait safely inside for casting. Up the centre of the lead nose is a hole that allows water to rush up on impact and eject the lid, which in turn allows the bait to fall out. There is no doubt that the Baitsafe gives absolutely perfect presentation no matter how soft the bait, something that can be just about impossible to do with conventional terminal tackle, even with a 'hook-up' device, when you need to cast long distances.

As for Baitsafe's casting ability, well it obviously is not going to be as good as a conventional bomb shaped sinker but it can still be cast over 150 yards if necessary. One thing to watch though on the casting front is that because it has a much greater surface area than a small sinker it tends to swing much slower during the preliminary build up to the cast and therefore you have to adjust your timing to suit. A bonus however of this larger surface area is that the Baitsafe planes to the surface very quickly once you start to reel in and therefore is ideal for venues which see rocks, weed or large amounts of lost tackle in the first 80 yards or so from the shoreline.

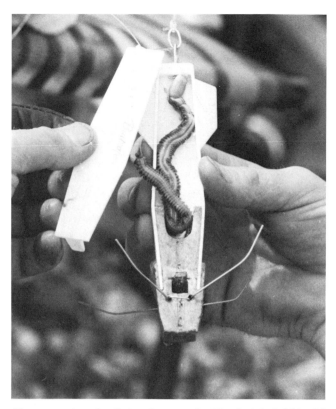

Above—using the Baitsafe capsule. The bait is laid inside the body.

Below—once closed the lid protects the bait from casting whiplash and wind drag.

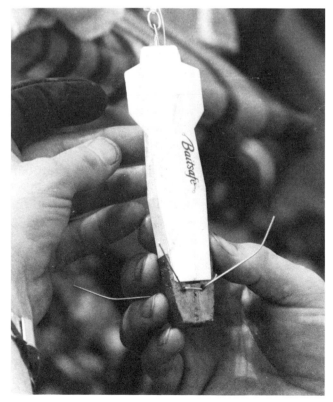

Hooks

Considering the fact that the hook is probably the most important single item of terminal tackle because it is this that attaches the fish to your line, many anglers do not treat it with the respect it deserves. Many anglers simply walk into their local tackle shop and ask for a dozen 'whiting hooks' or a dozen 'cod hooks' and leave the final selection to the dealer. Often the dealer is knowledgeable enough to give his customer a reasonable hook but sometimes you are likely to get palmed off with whatever is easiest to reach or those old stock that he just has not been able to shift.

By walking out with something second rate you will have immediately reduced your chances of landing fish before you even cast out. I know that sea fish are considered to be pretty thick and I've seen them caught on hooks that look as if they have been borrowed from the local butcher's shop but usually that is on those odd days when they tend to be feeding almost suicidally. In years gone by when fish were much more prolific than they are now you would probably manage to take home a relatively good catch no matter what hook you used or its condition. If you had fifteen bites you may have taken ten fish but now you may only get five and if the fish are a bit finicky they could be the five you miss.

Match fishing in particular is an area where you just cannot afford to lose any fish or miss any bites at all. Often the difference between finishing in the prizes or just missing out is those odd fish or two and I have lost count of the time that I've heard anglers complaining 'Just couldn't hook them', or 'Dropped off halfway in' at the weigh in. You will never be 100% successful and you will always miss a few bites and lose a few fish no matter how competent an angler you are or how careful you are with your hook choice. You can, however, reduce these happenings to the barest minimum by selecting your hook to match the species of fish you are after and the conditions you fish under and then preparing and maintaining it as well as you can.

HOOK DESIGN

Firms like the Norwegian Mustad company and even Britain's own Partridge concern list absolutely hundreds of different hooks for all types of fishing. Even taking the sea angling hooks as a separate issue the range is quite incredible, and by adding those offered by the host of smaller manufacturers it is no wonder that many anglers find it all a bit confusing. Finishes vary from silver, gold, blued and bronzed, materials include ordinary steel wire, stainless steel and high carbon steel; points can be hollow, curved-in, knife edge or superior. The list goes on and on but just how much difference these variations mean in terms of the capture of more fish is debatable although most people have their favourites.

All hooks are constructed from steel wire with the final shape and strength often depending on the manufacturing process. Some hooks will be made from stainless steel wire which is supposed to give added corrosion resistance, but usually they are the heavier forged type more suited to boat fishing. Others use steels that have a high percentage of carbon in them which makes the hook appear very hard and strong for a given size. The problem is that these hooks tend to be very brittle and prone to sudden breakage rather than bending once they have been strained beyond their design limits. The same can be said of the standard wire hooks if they have been over tempered which also results in a brittle hook. Tempering is a heat treating process carried out on steel to give it added strength and although it is desirable to give the hook additional strength care has to be taken not to overdo it.

A compromise has to be reached between the strong, hard hook that has a tendency to snap and the softer temper of the hook which will straighten out rather than break. The weakest point on the hook's body is where the cut has been made into the steel to form the barb and the last thing you want is for the hook to break off here on the 'strike'. This is more likely to happen if the point hits a bone because once in contact with soft flesh it should slide in down to the bend where most of the strain will then be taken. This is the place where I have found many high carbon steel hooks and those which are over tempered tend to break and therefore I choose hooks with a bit more spring in them, which will distort if over-stressed rather than snap. The point is that it is possible to land a fish on a hook that has bent a bit but not on one that has broken.

Whatever type of steel wire used hooks can be divided into two main types; round wire and forged wire. The round wire needs no further explanation but forging is a process where the wire is flattened slightly and gives additional strength to the hook. A forged hook will, roughly speaking, be equivalent in strength to the next size larger in round wire. Usually the forging is limited to the lower end of the shank and the bend of the hook, the areas where most strain occurs.

The strength of the hook will also depend on the gauge of wire used. Most manufacturers use what they call a 'standard' wire for each size of hook and then use either a heavier gauge for very strong hooks or a thinner gauge for lighter patterns. The terms 2 × finer or 2 × heavy are sometimes seen in catalogues and these mean that the hooks have been made out of wire which is finer or heavier than standard. A hook which is 2 × fine is made out of wire which would be standard for a hook two sizes smaller i.e., a size 2 which is 2 × fine is made from the wire of a standard size 4. Rather than getting too involved with technicalities you will soon notice the difference by eye and from a strength rating viewpoint you have forged hooks, standard wire hooks and extra fine wire hooks.

The way that the hook is formed or its final shape is often the point that makes an angler buy it rather than another one. A typical example is those terrible 'beak' hooks with the sliced shank because these are awful hooks yet I've been told that they actually out-sell every other design. Why this should be I just can't imagine because they are made from a heavy gauge wire which is far too strong for just about anything that swims in our waters. They have those useless slices in the shank which are supposed to hold the bait on the hook yet are so sharp that they would only slice it to pieces, and they have that awful curved in point.

Whether the shape actually does have anything to do with its effectiveness I don't know but there certainly isn't one that has proved to have a measurable advantage. Personally I like a hook with quite a deep throat yet I use round bend hooks quite often and these have a fairly shallow throat. They seem just as good but the deeper throat looks to have a better holding power once the fish is hooked. Also a twist in the bend so that the point is offset looks better rather than a hook where the point is in line with the shank. Hooks formed in this manner are known as *kirbed* if the twist is to the right and *reversed* if the twist is to the left looking at the hook straight on with the eye uppermost. Some of the matchmen I know feel sure the offset point is better and even put their own set into models which don't have them as standard.

What about the point itself? There are six different types of point, the hollow, superior, curved-in, dublin, knife edge and of course barbless. By far the most common are the superior and the hollow with the barbless being very good for freshwater but of no practical use from the shore. The superior point is the standard flattened point seen on most forged hooks and some wire ones. The hollow point refers to it being hollow ground forming a circular needle like point which is most commonly seen on wire hooks. Straight from the packet the hollow points are certainly the sharpest but can be difficult to keep that way. This is because they taper quite steeply, which means that the amount of material that has to be removed to retain the point gets greater as you move back towards the barb. The superior point may come out of the packet quite blunt but being a relatively long, flat and quite thin point it is easily sharpened up with a stone and more importantly easily kept sharp during the fishing session.

Exactly how sharp a hook should be is another thing that is open to debate. A really thin, incredibly sharp point is fine when you test it against your finger but useless after one cast from the beach. As soon as you reel it in through even fine sand and shingle the tip of the point will get bent over. However the point should always be as sharp as realistically possible and I use a small rotary grinder to remove some of the metal between the point and the barb. Many hooks are just too 'meaty' in this area and by removing some metal the point can continuously be kept sharp. Be careful not to overdo it otherwsie you will end up with the blunting problem already mentioned and check its sharpness after every cast.

Finally we come to finish. As mentioned earlier hooks come in a variety of finishes and the idea of these is to resist the effects of rust and corrosion. Stainless steel is obviously the best in this respect although the range available is quite limited. Really though the points wear away before the hook rusts that badly and therefore I have never found any use for stainless hooks. Plated hooks in silver, gold, blued and bronzed offer enough resistance to corrosion and their life is more likely to be shortened by an underwater obstruction rather than rust. Some anglers particularly prefer a certain colour, perhaps blued or bronzed so the hook doesn't stand out while others actually want it to and choose silver or gold to attract. One angler I know swears by gold hooks for flatfish but I've found no particular advantages with any type. Usually the bait covers it up anyway and the fish can't see it.

CHOOSING A HOOK

For shore fishing you can divide your hooks into two sections (a) wire hooks for most general species and conditions and (b) forged hooks for heavy duty work. Within these broad classifications there are several different patterns from which you can choose and each has its advantages and disadvantages. The important thing for you as the angler is to look at them and decide which one will best cover your needs. The barest requirement is that it is strong enough but don't go overboard and use coarse, heavy hooks particularly if they feature prominent barbs. Hooks such as this usually only result in second rate bait presentation and hooking ability.

Most wire hooks are based on the now famous Aberdeen pattern and really you wouldn't go far wrong if you stick to these for all your fishing. They offer a very good compromise between bait presentation, hooking ability and strength which is exactly what a good hook should do. Mustad offer two types, the standard wire and the extra fine wire blued. The extra fine wire hooks code 3730A are ideal for smaller species such as flatfish, pouting and whiting and are probably the most desirable hook for match anglers to use for these fish. This is because they are very thin in the wire allowing perfect presentation of delicate baits such as harbour and white ragworm. They have a long slim point which can be made super sharp to hook a fish as soon as it breathes on the bait and finally their lightness allows small fish to suck them right in without encountering too much resistance.

Although fine wire blues are available in sizes up to 3/0 I prefer to stick to those below 1/0. Any fish requiring a hook bigger than that really needs a stronger hook. I have seen quite good cod landed on them but really using these is pushing your luck that bit far. Unfortunately the blues are only available in plain shanks and therefore they have to be whipped by you or the dealer and you can pay dearly for the latter. The shanks are incredibly long, about the longest I've seen and therefore it pays to cut them down to about two thirds of their original length. Personally I just don't like that amount of metal inside a bait meant for small fish but some anglers actually prefer it.

For those of you interested in whipping blues or any other hook come to that it is a very simple if laborious task. Firstly cut your shank to the required length with pliers or similar and then round off the sharp end with a file. Be sure to do this because the cutting process leaves a knife edge and once I did some hooks and omitted to file the ends. As a result I hooked a cod, brought it all the way in and then it was turned over in the surf, promptly cutting clean through the snood; a lesson learnt the hard way. Next cut your snood line to length and put a simple overhand knot in it. Lay the line against the hook shank with the knot quite close to the start of the bend. Whip along the shank to a point just past the knot, trim off the ends and then smother the whipping in either Araldite or Superglue. Superglue is the quickest and easiest but Araldite gives a nicer glossy coat.

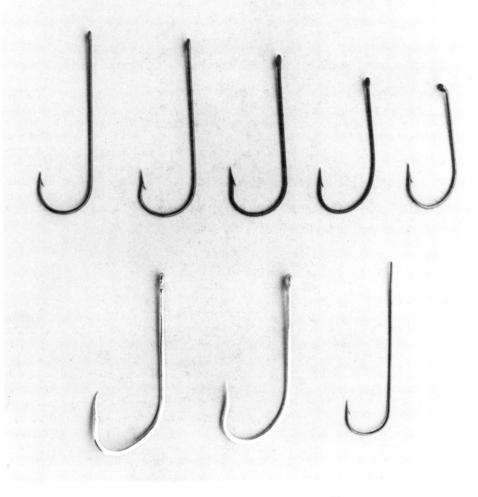

Shorefishing hooks. Top row – Partridge Aberdeen, Mustad Aberdeen, Sundridge Aberdeen, Breakaway Spearpoint, Mustad 79510, Bottom row – Mustad 'Beak' (to be avoided!), Mustad Viking, Mustad extra fine wire blue.

A small modification but one that is quite useful when using worm baits is to incorporate a small spur onto the shank. This is simply done by whipping the shank as before but only as far as the knot. The piece of line past the knot is then turned back to face back up the shank and the whipping continued. Clip the piece of line to leave about $\frac{1}{4}$ inch sticking out and this forms the retaining spur. Keeping baits on the hook is always a problem for the shore angler particularly for those casting long distances and anything that helps had to be an advantage.

If you don't fancy a hook whipping session then you may like to try the Partridge fine wire match hooks labelled under the code Z9 A. These hooks are eyed but have a very much shorter shank and smaller barb than the Mustad hooks. The point is also quite short and being hollow ground it can be difficult to re-shapen as effectively as the longer flat point of the blue. Another consideration is that the Partridge company use fairly high carbon steels for their hooks and in very thin wires such as these they are likely to snap if over strained. The thing to remember though with any of these ultra-hooks is that their use should be limited to occasions when the chance of fish over about 4 pounds is nil. Otherwise a very gentle hand will be called for.

Moving up to the standard wire Aberdeens you have a hook that will land most round fish such as cod and bass over clean ground in all but very rough seas as long as you do not adopt the 'hope and heave' approach. The Mustad version (code 3282) is a reasonably soft hook that will bend rather than break and is my favourite in any size between 2 and 6/0 for any species. The points are nicely long and re-sharpen very well and although at one time I thought that the shanks were too long and cut and whipped them, I don't bother now yet catch just as many fish.

Slightly stiffer wired are the Partridge Aberdeens (code Z10) which in a similar manner to its fine wire cousin has the tendency to snap rather than bend. The same can be said for the Au Lion D'or Aberdeens (code 1322) which are probably the strongest of the three. Although they also break rather than bend, the amount of pressure required to do this is considerable and more than a shore

angler should ever put on his fish. Both models have hollow ground points which I have commented on earlier.

The area in which I carry out most of my fishing rarely calls for the use of a forged hook. Even when I do find it necessary the relatively fine wired type such as the Mustad 79510 are all that are necessary. The 79510 has received a great deal of praise over the years and it is the one I tend to use. Its general shape, wire thickness, barb, point and near perfect shank length make it excellent for shore angling particularly now that it is available with a straight eye rather than the older turned in eye. Sometimes it is a case of striking a compromise between size and strength. You may be fishing for mainly small fish but there is the definite chance of a cod or bass. At times such as this I would use a very sharp size 1 or 1/0 79510 so that small fish could be hooked but large fish could also be landed. The other time that I would go for a forged hook is in very rough seas when the undertow behind the surf puts a terrific strain on the hook in the final stages of the fight. Even though 5/0 and 6/0 Aberdeens are quite strong I prefer the added security of a forged hook in case a 20 pounder turns up.

If however you are likely to catch conger or rays which chew up anything less than a man sized hook you will need to move up to the Mustad Viking range or the Sundridge Sea Specimens. With these fish, bait size is likely to be fairly substantial anyway and the hook weight will be relatively unimportant. Also the bottom is likely to be unfriendly at the best and hauling large fish calls for a very strong hook not to mention the rest of the tackle.

Choosing the best hook for the job becomes increasingly easy as you gain experience but the main things to realise are that the size should be chosen for the fish you are after, the size of bait you are using and kept sharp at all times. When fishing at long range the fish hook themselves and you must make sure that you make it as easy as possible for them to succeed. Heavy, blunt hooks will make sure that you fail miserably. To help you then I have constructed this chart which shows the hooks I use and their good and bad features.

Hook Type	Advantages	Disadvantages	Species & Conditions
Mustad 3730A extra fine wire blued	Light weight. Long point, easily sharpened.	Has to be whipped. Only tolerates limited strain before bending.	Whiting, pouting, flatfish in most conditions. Small codling & bass in moderate seas.
Partridge Z9A extra fine wire	Light weight. Eyed. Small neat barb. Short shank.	Difficult to keep sharp. Tends to snap rather than bend.	As above.

Hook Type	Advantages	Disadvantages	Species & Conditions
Mustad 3282 fine wire	Long flat point. Easy to bait with worms. Easy to keep sharp. Bends under severe strain.	Shank very long in larger sizes.	Small/medium size fish in any conditions. Large fish in calm/moderate seas & clean ground.
Partridge Z10 fine wire	Slightly stronger than 3282. Small neat barb.	Difficult to re-sharpen. Will snap rather than bend when over strained.	As above.
Au Lion D'or 1322	Stronger than both 3282 & Z10	As above, but will withstand greater strain before breaking.	As above but will handle most species over clean ground in any seas.
Mustad 79510 forged	Light weight. Long thin point. Good shank length. Quite strong.	None.	Just about anything apart from very small fish or very large strong jawed fish like conger.
Mustad Viking	Very strong. Available in stainless if required.	A bit heavy & coarse for anything but large fish.	Large fish only. Any conditions.

Terminal Tackle

The way that a freshwater angler presents his baited hook to the fish can make all the difference between success and failure. This is particularly the case on some of the more popular venues where the fish are likely to have felt the hook several times and therefore anything that does not act in a natural manner will be viewed with suspicion. There are of course those 'mad' days when the fish seem to take anything vaguely edible but if you relied on those days to catch fish you would end up with a dry net more often than not.

Most sea fish on the other hand get only one chance and no more, so the need for such precision is usually unnecessary. One only has to witness the vast hauls taken on commercial long lines, which must represent the crudest terminal tackle possible with their thick lines and coarse hooks. Part of the reason for their effectiveness must be that they are set in areas where there are large numbers of fish and therefore keen competition for food. Further inshore this competition is likely to be lessened and therefore the fish will probably exercise a bit more caution when inspecting an attractive item.

Functions If you took a cross section of sea anglers in this country and asked them to produce a terminal rig for a particular venue and a particular species I am sure you would have several variations. All of them would probably work well if it was simply a matter of lowering them onto the feeding fish or casting a very short distance. As the required casting distance increased so the number of effective set-ups would reduce, because as distance increases the terminal tackle has to be far more exact to work well. Small points which hardly matter at casting ranges of up to 100 yds suddenly become very important when you are looking at ranges of 140 yards plus. There is no doubt that the increasing need for distance casting has influenced the design of terminal tackle more than any other single point.

At this stage it is as well to look at the basic functions that you want your terminal tackle to carry out. Firstly it should present the bait where the fish are, i.e., the sea bed; secondly it should present the bait in a manner that allows the fish to pick it up easily and swallow; thirdly it should transmit the signal of a biting fish to the angler; and fourthly it should carry the bait the required distance, arriving there in good condition. The aim of the angler must be to fulfil all of these functions with as simple a set-up as possible; each item used to make up the tackle should have a purpose.

Judging by some of the weird and wonderful Christmas tree rigs I've seen fly seawards it is apparent that some anglers have never really thought about any of the tasks that their trace is trying to do.

Presenting the bait to the fish near the sea bed is really no problem at all because you only need to ensure that the hooks are placed quite close to the sinker. With multi-hook paternoster traces some anglers think that the baits were being offered at varying distances off the bottom but this is not true. When beach fishing even from steep venues a minimum of twenty to thirty yards of line immediately above the sinker will be lying on the sea bed so that's where your baits will be. The only way that you are likely to be able to fish above the sea bed is from a pier or harbour wall and even then you would have to fish at relatively short range. More often than not if the fish do seem to prefer one particular hook it is the one nearest the sinker and therefore the one 'nailed' to the bottom hardest.

Personally I do not think that you need to go overboard in trying to make the bait act or look natural because in the very limited visibility of our coastal waters smell and taste are far more important. Lugworm are seldom seen floating about in bunches or for that fact in very close company with a silver ragworm or slivers of mackerel and peeler crab are not normally bound up like a neat little parcel with elasticated thread. Fresh bait that smells right is all that is necessary to catch fish.

Long hook lengths are supposed to allow the bait to move about more and sometimes they can be effective, particularly with flatfish. In general however I find that shorter hook lengths are equally as effective with additional movement being allowed by using a short spiked sinker or plain bomb if necessary. Long hook lengths are more prone to tangling anyway thereby reducing movement to the same or even less than short hook lengths. Worse still the bait could be buried in a mass of nylon making it impossible for the fish to pick up and swallow. As long as the hook length allows the fish to swallow the bait that is enough and here the species of fish can make a difference. Small fish such as whiting, pouting and flatfish are adequately handled with fairly short hook lengths and I have never found the need to use much more than 6–10 inches. Larger fish such as cod and bass may require a bit more to ensure that the bait is well inside the mouth to give a secure hook hold. Even so, 15–18 inches should be ample and used

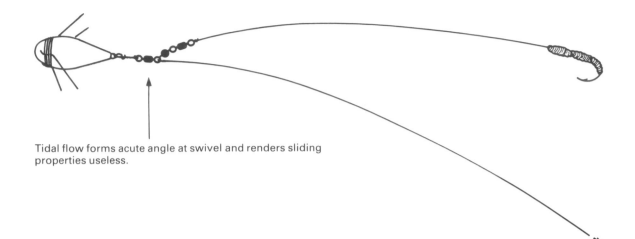

Tidal flow forms acute angle at swivel and renders sliding properties useless.

on a single hook paternoster would remain tangle free.

One of the major reasons that running leger traces are still used is that some anglers stick rigidly to the principal that the bite is transmitted more positively to the rod tip. If the line ran perfectly straight from the rod tip to the bait then I would agree but under practical fishing conditions this is rarely the case. At most venues there is a tidal flow that runs parallel to the shoreline with a fair amount of force. Therefore once the sinker has anchored itself into the bottom the water pressure will be acting on the bait and on the main line. The latter will be formed into a bow coming away from the sinker almost parallel to the bait (see diagram). The line will form a very acute angle at the sinker and even if you use a porcelain eyed swivel, or other gadget like a small boom, the friction at this point will not allow the line to move cleanly. Even if it does move slightly the main line bow will absorb it and the only way a bite will show up is to shift the sinker slightly. This is what a straightforward paternoster does anyway so you have absolutely no advantages, particularly considering the fact that a flowing trace will probably have tangled itself up during the cast and it is casting ability that influences trace design more than any other point.

Long range casting produces no end of problems for the angler to overcome if he is still to fish effectively. Firstly the trace has got to be fairly streamlined if it is going to cast well and therefore wind resisting metal booms and long flowing traces are out. They may fish very well and up to ranges of about 100 yards can still be considered but the further you get above that figure the worse they become. It is useless having a good fish-catching trace if it is going to fall well short of the feeding area; even a relatively poorly presented

PATERNOSTER FOR ROUGH GROUND

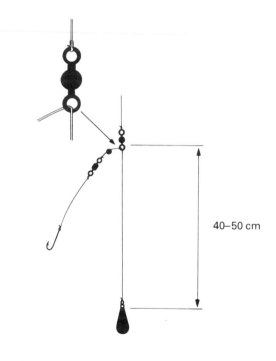

40–50 cm

PATERNOSTER WITH FISH ON

Rod pulls one way and fish the other resulting in sinker clearing the bottom.

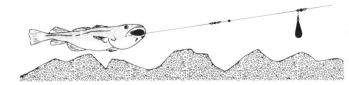

bait is going to stand a better chance of being taken if it reaches the right place.

Secondly, the high sinker speeds necessary for distance can literally disintegrate soft baits without being helped by the whiplash effect of long, free hanging hook lengths. Slimhooks and careful baiting up are part of the answer but a well designed trace is the rest.

The biggest aid to long range casting as far as terminal tackle is concerned is the use of the bait clip. Bait clips are a relatively new idea and one which is now taken for granted by most casters in this country. It consists of a small length of wire bent as shown in the photograph or even a small hook with the barb broken off. This is then secured to the leader by a short length of wire sheathing or the plastic ledger stops that freshwater anglers use. The idea is that the hook complete with bait is held tightly against the trace as the cast is made thereby eliminating any whiplash. Once the trace hits the sea the momentory slackness of the line allows the hook and bait to fall free thereby arriving on the sea bed in good condition and untangled.

The choice however comes in whether you decide to 'hook-up' or 'hook-down', that is place the bait clip above or below the point where the hook length joins the main line. With the bait clip placed above ('hook-up'), the wind pressure keeps the bait pushed firmly on the hook as the trace flies out to sea but there is a much greater chance that the bait will become dislodged and tangle. Also with large baits the distance between bait and sinker can be enough to upset the flight, inducing 'wobble' and consequently a loss of distance. With the bait clip below ('hook down'), the bait can be placed right behind the sinker, in its slipstream so to speak, which allows it to fly much truer. However the wind pressure will be doing its best to push the bait away from the hook and it is necessary to place a stop knot on the hook length to avoid this. Otherwise the fish will be swallowing the line instead of the hook and you will miss them. Personally I always hook-down but both ways seem to work well, certainly better than not using them at all. For fixed-spool users they are essential because the 'twang' produced on line release will remove most of the bait from the hook if you let it hang free. With multipliers the release is much smoother but even so I consider bait clips essential for all distances above 120 yards.

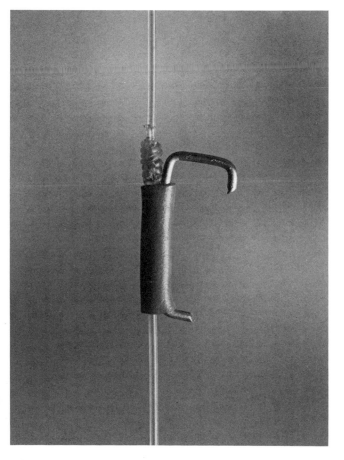

A bait clip. Simply a bent piece of wire and a short length of electrical wire sheathing but an essential part of any long distance trace.

Traces

The idea then is to produce neat, simple traces that do the job with the minimum of components and there is no doubt that the simple paternoster is the one to use. It is quick and easy to make, casts extremely well and ensures that the bait is 'nailed' to the sea bed. You can use either single hook, two hook or three hook variations depending on conditions, bait selection and the species you are trying to catch, i.e. single hook for big fish or bad conditions, three hooks for flats, whiting and match fishing.

As far as components are concerned you really only need a length of heavy line, a couple of oval split rings and a piece of wire and plastic flex for the bait clip. Safety is obviously a major consideration when it comes to distance casting and therefore I use a trace line 5–10 lb BS heavier than that used for the leader. That allows for the multitude of knots which will obviously reduce the line's breaking strain and the fact that the trace is going to be the part of line to get the most abrasion during reeling in. The same point must be considered with swivels if you want to use them although for leader and lead attachment they are totally unnecessary. Always buy high quality swivels such as Berkley and beware of many of the snap type, swivel/links that use fine wire, as they can gradually cut their way through leader line and sometimes open out. I use oval split rings exclusively because they are very cheap and absolutely reliable which is all you need to ask of terminal tackle components.

The area where most anglers traces vary is the

THREE HOOK PATERNOSTER

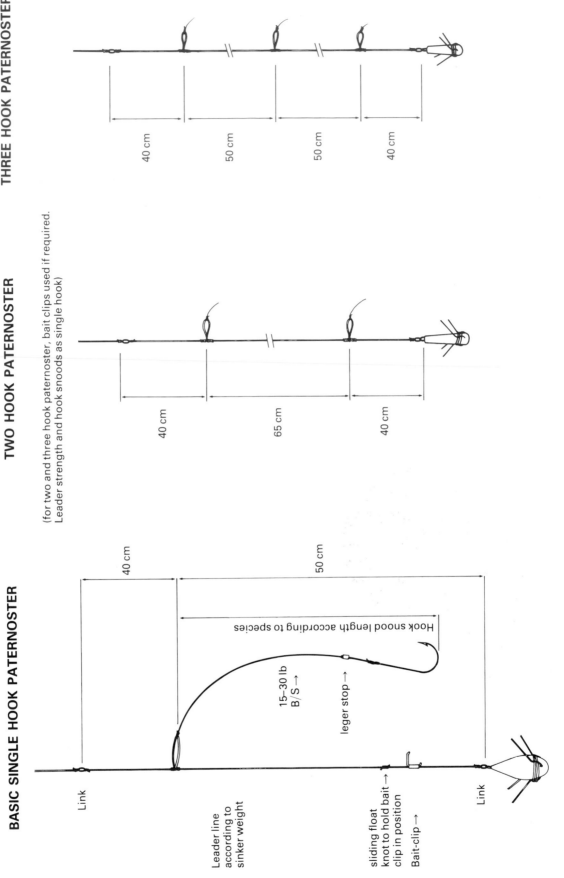

40 cm

50 cm

50 cm

40 cm

TWO HOOK PATERNOSTER

(for two and three hook paternoster, bait clips used if required. Leader strength and hook snoods as single hook)

40 cm

65 cm

40 cm

BASIC SINGLE HOOK PATERNOSTER

40 cm

50 cm

Hook snood length according to species

15–30 lb B/S →

leger stop →

Link

Leader line according to sinker weight

sliding float knot to hold bait clip in position

Bait-clip →

Link

54

method they use to attach the hook length to the heavy line. Really, as long as you keep the hook lengths spaced far enough apart and they do not tangle up easily that is all that matters but every angler has his favourite method so I will run through some and let you make up your own mind.

(1) Blood Loop This is the basis of just about every paternoster and the simplest. Just tie a blood loop in the trace line at the positions you want, leaving a loop approximately one inch long. Attach the hook length to the end of the loop.

(2) Blood Loop with Plastic Flex To hold the hook link further away from the trace line and thereby reduce the tangle risk tie a blood loop with the loop itself about 2–3 inches long. Cut a piece of electrical flex covering a bit shorter than that and then slip it over the loop. This forms a short stiff 'boom' and its 'stiffness' can be improved by running some glue around the end of the flex where it butts up to the blood knot.

(3) Twisted Blood Loop This again holds the hook line further from the trace line. Tie a blood loop with the loop 2–3 inches long. Get a length of wire with one end hooked and engage that end with the end of the loop. Turn the wire so that it gradually 'winds-up' the loop rather like the rubber band of a model aircraft, then holding straight pour some boiling water over the line. Cool it off under the cold tap and you will find that the twist stays in the loop. Alternatively you can put the twist into the loop before tying the knot by forming the loop, turn the ends in opposite directions until the loop has enough twists in it then tie the knot as usual.

(4) Cut Blood Loop Sometimes referred to as the straight-through trace you tie a blood loop with the loop again about 3 inches long. Then cut one end near the knot itself so that there is a single length of the heavy line joined at the knot. The hook length is attached to the trace by using a leader knot and the piece of trace line helps to hold the hook length clear.

(5) Captive Swivel Slide a swivel with a small bead either side of it onto the trace line, then tie a blood loop at the position where the hook/trace attachment is to be. Trim the loop leaving a knot on the trace line and rest the beads and swivel against it. Tie another knot the other side of the swivel and beads so that they are held within an area of 2–3 inches of the trace line. This is a very popular method of attachment and was particularly successful before bait clips. Then with the bait swinging freely it would tend to 'helicopter' as it flew out to sea and could tangle. The swivel allowed it to turn freely thereby reducing tangles and presenting the bait better. With bait clips this is less likely but the method of attachment is still widely used.

ALTERNATIVE HOOK SNOOD/TRACE CONNECTIONS FOR PATERNOSTER TERMINAL TACKLE

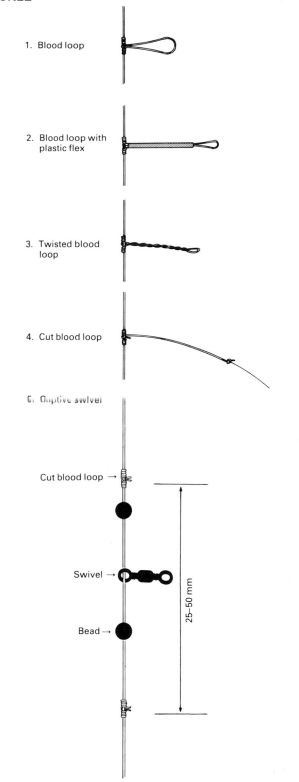

1. Blood loop

2. Blood loop with plastic flex

3. Twisted blood loop

4. Cut blood loop

5. Captive swivel

Cut blood loop →

Swivel →

Bead →

25–50 mm

Note: Instead of cut blood-loops, sliding float knots can be used. These allow the hook position relative to the sinker to be varied. Sometimes fish show a preference for baits close to the sinker and vice-versa.

Hook Snoods In areas where there is a distinct chance of your terminal tackle becoming snagged such as rocky and/or weedy ground it is an advantage to use a hook snood of a lower breaking strain than the main line. Then if the hook gets snagged it is possible to break off without losing the rest of the terminal tackle. In such cases as this the main line is likely to be fairly substantial (over 25 lb BS) and therefore the hook can still be strong enough (20 lb BS) to land a decent fish in a heavy sea. Naturally the heavier the main line the greater the reduction in ultimate distance but in areas of rocks and weed long casting is seldom required.

Over clean ground where 12–15 lb BS line is adequate the use of even lighter hook snoods, in case of snagging, is not really a practical proposition. Very light lines (less than 12 lb BS) tend to tangle easily, particularly with fish such as whiting and pouting which tend to spin on the retrieve and are easily damaged. Most round fish have those very small needle-like teeth that rasp at the line severely reducing its overall breaking strain. Add to that those bait stealing monsters called crabs continually snatching at the bait with their claws and it's no wonder that you sometimes reel in with no hook on either!

To overcome these problems the hook snood really needs to be at least 20 lb BS even for small species so that it stands nicely clear of the main trace line. For codding I usually go for line in the 25–30 lb range having tried lighter hook lengths and found no advantage, quite the contrary in fact. In fast tides the water immediately above the bottom is always coloured even if the above layers are quite clear and therefore the fish are not likely to be spooked by thick line. Mind you I usually use Gantel for both traces and hook snoods because its yellow colouring is very well hidden against a sandy background and it may make a difference at times. To be honest I don't really think it does but confidence is a very important feature in all forms of angling.

The length of the hook snood is often a matter of personal preference but some thought should be given to conditions and the species being sought. Small fish such as whiting, pouting and flatfish should be handled with fairly short snoods in the 6–10 inch range while larger fish may need that bit extra to get the bait well inside their mouths, say 12–15 inches. I find these lengths successful on the majority of occasions but fish are funny creatures and at times show a preference that defies explanation. It pays therefore never to lay down hard and fast rules about anything to do with angling so

Fish like these whiting are comfortably handled on quite short hook lengths.

although you need some basis to begin with be prepared to experiment. Some days the fish seem to prefer a bait that is virtually 'nailed' to the bottom and on others one that moves attractively in the tide on a long hook snood. That is the nice thing with bait clips, you can use virtually any snood length but retain streamlined casting properties.

The hooks need to be suited to the species of fish and the bait size. In the chapter about hooks I described the types of hooks to use but the size needs to be selected on the above factors. Unlike freshwater fish, sea fish are very rarely hook shy and if the bait is right they are not going to let a small piece of metal get in the way! Fine wires are ideal in sizes 4–1/0 for flatfish, 1–3/0 for medium size round fish such as whiting and codling and 3/0–6/0 for larger cod and bass. At one time I considered 3/0 a fairly large hook and usually used it for cod but in the quest for a higher bite/hooking success I tried larger hooks and multiple hooks. The best results came with one large 6/0 hook and a compact bait because not only did nearly every bite result in a hooked fish but the number of smaller fish caught seemed to increase rather than reduce, so they were hardly hook shy!

For most pleasure sessions I stick to one large hook but there are times when different arrangements can work. In matches the angler is concerned with catching as many sizeable fish as possible, no matter what the species and he will probably want to try a selection of baits. This can be done with a standard two-hook paternoster but a single-hook paternoster rig equipped with a wishbone snood can be more successful. Two fairly small, say 2/0 hooks are placed side by side as shown in the diagram and each can be baited with the same or different baits. The advantage is that although the baits are fished like a cocktail each has its own hook in case a preference is shown and should a big fish turn up it will probably swallow both anyway!

Another plus point is that a small fish may get hooked on one leaving the other free in case a big fish comes along and swallows the lot. This happens quite often when the cod shoals move in at the end of the autumn and there are still large numbers of whiting about. Purposely fishing a livebait is a good way of picking up the better cod because such fish are usually well into double figures. Naturally a whiting can't be cast far so you have to catch it out to sea and by using the rig shown you have a pretty good chance of hooking both a whiting and then hopefully a big cod. Some anglers use the larger hook above the smaller one but sometimes the cod do not swallow the whiting far enough and miss the big hook. This way it should take both. By the way, only bait the small hook otherwise you will end up with two whiting!

WISHBONE SNOOD

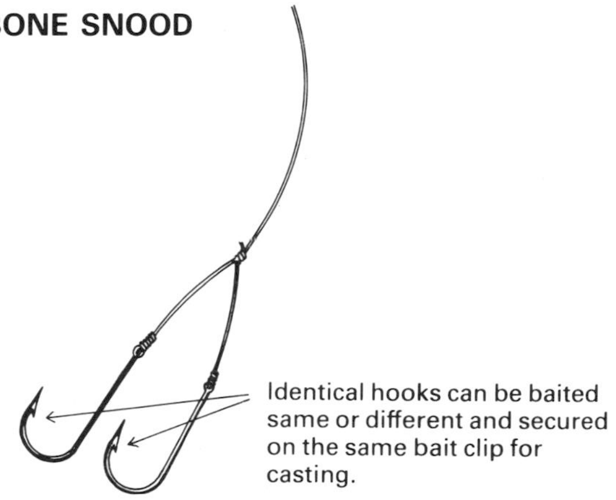

Identical hooks can be baited same or different and secured on the same bait clip for casting.

LIVEBAIT SNOOD

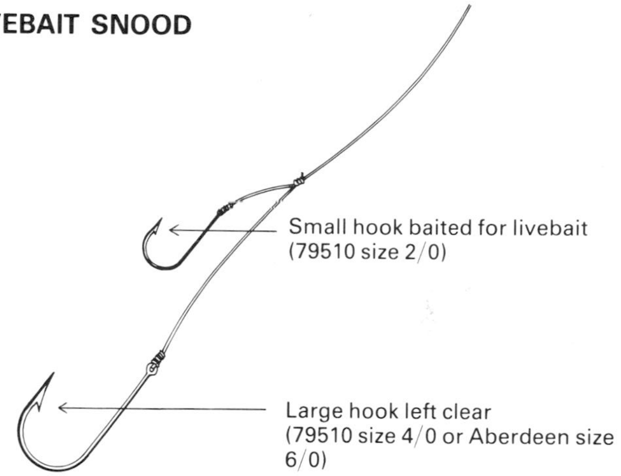

Small hook baited for livebait (79510 size 2/0)

Large hook left clear (79510 size 4/0 or Aberdeen size 6/0)

Casting Techniques

Being able to cast a baited trace out to sea is the basic requirement for any shore angler. Ultimately this could be as far as modern tackle will allow or at the other extreme 20 yards, whichever was deemed necessary to catch fish. For the majority of shore anglers in this country the upper limit is the one that provides the most problems because on average their maximum range is way short of this mark. In past years it seemed as though there were enough fish about to keep the majority happy and the necessity for distance casting was not apparent. Now however the situation is very different due to a very efficient fleet that is doing their best to take everything that swims. With reduced numbers and therefore without such keen competition for food, the fish are no longer forced to comb the sea bed right up to the shoreline. Instead smaller shoals run through at ranges which are often outside the average cast and therefore the need to be able to cast that bit further has become much more important.

Advantages of Distance Casting During the sixties Leslie Moncrieff was given a great amount of publicity in the angling press because of the huge hauls of cod he had taken from the beach at Dungeness. The basis of his success, apart from the obvious right place at the right time, was the ability to put a good sized bait well out from the shoreline. Really that was the beginning of the distance casting philosophy and since then many journalists have written on the subject. Certainly there has been no shortage of advice on rods, reels and techniques for those prepared to read and it was from this source that I obtained the basic knowledge from which my own casting skills have developed. It seems that many anglers throughout the country however are just not interested or cannot believe the advantages distance casting can give them. On average the overall casting standard is very poor and I would be surprised if it worked out more than a meagre 80 yds or so.

At this range you are limited to a very narrow band of water close to the shore line and have to rely heavily on the fish actually moving in that close. Mind you it doesn't seem to bother many because their usual reply is "I don't need to cast further. I get plenty of fish as it is". This reply is very interesting and the immediate reaction is just how many is plenty? One, two, six or ten fish in a session? Although some anglers are content with only a few fish I am sure that the majority would like to catch more yet are not aware of the advan-

tages additional casting range could give. As far as they are concerned if they are not catching then the fish are not feeding – it is as simple as that. Fishing techniques are vitally important, there is no doubt about that, but very often it is just plain distance that decides a good catch or nothing. Often I have fished a popular venue and taken several cod whilst those around have the odd one or two. Everybody has been using lugworm so there is no secret bait and traces have been virtually identical. The only difference has been casting range yet when you pack up there is always someone quick to move in as though you have found the secret spot.

It is not as though tournament type distances are necessary either because often a consistant 120–130 yds would have put them among the fish. Although individual beaches differ in their characteristics it is surprising the number of venues where this distance seems to be the optimum. There are always the close in and absolute distance venues but features such as gullies and banks are very often located around the 120–130 yd mark and it is here that you would expect the food and therefore fish to collect. From their position on the beach the 80 yd man probably thinks that he is close enough but take a look at a measured 40 yds and you will soon see that it is more than enough to make a difference. Fish in the sea are not evenly spread about the bottom but just like those in a river or lake prefer areas where food collects naturally and that is the place to cast.

Some beaches have deep water only a relatively short way out and here fish often move closer in. These venues are pretty well known as a rule and tend to become very crowded at peak times. Such fishing conditions can get uncomfortable at times especially with any lateral tidal flow. Crossed lines are inevitable and I have never found it much fun having your tackle continually retrieved by a neighbour. Also the catch rate is bound to be lower because on any one tide there will only be a certain number of fish running the beach. The more people fishing, the more the fish will be shared out resulting in less for you. It is quite interesting to note that many really good catches are taken on days when there are relatively few other anglers fishing.

Night time is also supposed to bring the fish closer in but again brings the crowds. There is no doubt that many fish do venture further in during darkness because of the added security it gives them. Most popular venues in my area are absolutely packed on autumn and winter nights when the cod are 'in'. Arrive after six o'clock and it is very likely that you will not get a spot. Personally I am not very keen on night fishing, although I still do a fair bit, because it takes much of the enjoyment out of being by the sea and delighting in the surroundings. Casting, landing fish and just general fishing is so much nicer compared with the 'existing in a small circle of light that could be anywhere' feeling. At times night fishing really is the only way to get a good catch and the chance of a bigger fish is also increased but the potential is very often equalled in daylight if you have the casting ability to exploit it. Many of my best catches have come on the most beautiful, calm days when you would not have given yourself much chance at all.

Daylight fishing during periods of rough weather is best of all because the fish are quick to move in on the free food pounded out of the sand by strong swells. The very best time is usually taken as the first or second tide after the sea has calmed. However, part of the reason may be that Mr Average's 90 yds is quickly reduced to a meagre 50 yds by the onshore wind and at that range he has a fair chance of his terminal tackle being swept back up the beach. In these circumstances the good caster will still be clearing 100 yds, putting his baits past the breakers into the quieter water beyond. By taking care to keep his line clear of the wave tips he should be able to hold out well and take excellent catches while most anglers sit at home waiting for the storm to subside. Afterwards they may very well find the fish stuffed to the gills with all the free food and totally disinterested in any bait.

Quite honestly I could go on for ages quoting examples and reasons for learning to cast well but I hope that by now the point has sunk home. Long distance casting enables you to fish at times and venues often considered unprofitable by the majority of anglers and also take above average catches at those considered good. Linked with the watercraft and general fishing skills considered vital for a good angler it can make an excellent angler. This is a very important point to remember because although long, smooth and seemingly effortless casts are satisfying do not make the mistake of blasting out regardless. The competent angler knows when to lob a few yards and when to go flat out to catch fish most successfully.

Distance – The Target When the reverse taper rods first made their impact on the surfcasting scene the rage was to be able to cast a bait 100 yds although for the majority 70–80 yds was more realistic. Today with the stiff butt fast taper tip type of rod distances of 200 yds plus on the field and 150 yds with bait are quoted by some people as though it was run-of-the-mill. The trouble is that because tournament results have risen so dramatically the angler who has just bought the latest rod and reel automatically thinks that he is up there with the best. For many a cast on an accurate court would prove quite an upset.

Some angling journalists have not exactly helped matters either by talking of casting a bait 170 yds as though it were routine. Even when the first carbon beachcasters appeared advertisements implied that 220 yds plus on the field was easy yet the performance of these early models proved well short of the mark. I hope that during the discussion on rods I made it quite clear that the 'magic wand' does not exist. No rod will instantly transform your casting from mediocre to tournament standard without you putting in a lot of hard work. The very best you could expect would be an increase of say 30–40 yds if you had been using the most diabolical set-up possible and then changed to a well designed and 'tuned' outfit. Over the years I have been fortunate enough to try most surf rods and after the initial few casts there would only be about 5–10 yds between any of them. This is over grass and transferred to the beach the difference would be insignificant.

The question then comes down to just how far the average reasonably well co-ordinated person ought to be able to cast. Much depends on the sinker and bait size used – nobody would expect to cast half a herring as far as two or three small lugworm. Also line diameter plays a part, the thicker the running line the less distance you can hope to achieve, particularly with fixed-spool reels which are very sensitive to diameter change. As a standard, with a tournament style rod, 'tuned' reel, 0.35 mm running line, $5\frac{1}{4}$ oz sinker, streamlined paternoster, small bait, flat firm beach and steady tail wind I would expect something in the 190–210 yd region. In other words, that is the maximum in absolutely perfect conditions. In anything other than perfect conditions the distance would be down to 170–190 yds, dropping much lower in rough weather.

You may feel that this is an exaggeration but I can assure you that several casters in my area are as good and many others are not far behind. Experiments on the field have in fact shown slightly better results but I have allowed for the extra clothing and cold hands an angler has to put up with. On the other hand you may feel that for a 250 yd plus tournament caster, whose field and fishing techniques are virtually identical these distances are a bit less than expected. How can so much distance be lost? Well apart from the many factors of casting from a beach that affect distance the major consideration is the greatly increased wind resistance that a spiked sinker and baited trace puts up. Anybody who has studied physics will know that the law of diminishing returns works its worst with projected objects as the drag factors increase dramatically with each small increase in speed.

Some anglers tend to be under the impression that a cast of 200 yds only requires twice the effort of 100 yds but this is not the case. A cast of 150 yds would probably require twice the effort, but a 200 yd cast probably requires an increase of five to six times. Tournament results show the problem well because on days with no wind the difference separating the first few casters may be as little as a couple of yards, because each little bit requires a great deal of effort at that sort of range. In good conditions however the gap will widen and the difference may be as much as ten or even fifteen yards because the extra effort gains a greater advantage. By adding a spiked sinker and baited trace to the line the additional air resistance resembles the poorer conditions and when you start casting distances in excess of 150 yds considerable effort gives only small gains in distance. Casters that may be separated by 20 yds on the field probably find that only 10 yds separates their fishing distances in good weather and of course much less when it's bad.

With a well balanced and 'tuned' outfit and a reasonably well executed casting technique the average person should be able to reach 160–170 yds with a sinker alone. This standard should be enough to give you the 120–140 yds fishing range required, a distance seldom achieved although many like to think so. At this level only minimum practice is required, once you have got there, to keep in trim; it is only when you start looking for more, that regular practice sessions become essential. Really your own fishing situation will determine whether or not this is enough because some areas such as my native East Anglia are often notorious casting beaches. Also if you are a regular match competitor then that little bit extra distance is always nice if the fish prove reluctant to move inshore. If you are really keen then I would say that a field distance of 200 yds should give you all the distance you will ever need particularly when considering the problems that arise when even more power is applied. Spools full of wet line become increasingly difficult to grip with multiplier reels and with fixed-spool reels the extra power seems to increase the likelihood of a coil of line catching a ring. Also many baits just can't stand the initial acceleration of the sinker, no matter how well secured and just disintigrate. Let us then, put the target at a field distance of 175 yds – a realistic one which when achieved will increase your potential as a shore fisherman considerably.

Casting Basics With a modern fast taper rod there should be no problem in reaching about 120 yds simply by belting the rod as hard as possible with the conventional 'Overhead Thump' technique. Mind you a fixed-spool reel will have to be used, because a multiplier just would not stand such a short, sharp flick unless it was drastically over-braked. Once this level was reached however there would be virtually no improvement because the small rod arc such a technique produces can only put a limited amount of compression into the rod blank. Many anglers reach this stage and stay there simply because they just can't understand how any more power can be developed.

Alternatively you can take things nice and steady and by using the leg, back, shoulder and finally arm muscles to generate both speed and compression in the rod you can reach the same distance with comparative ease. Naturally the top tournament casters not only cast in this manner but they also hit the rod very hard as well because at their stage regular practice has made technique second nature. The problems with many would-be casters is that they start thrashing away once they have some idea on how it should be done because it is the only way they can think of to get further. Although difficult, some degree of self control must be exercised during this learning stage because casts of 150 yds require only a moderate amount of effort coupled with efficient technique. Unfortunately as with all things you only appreciate this fact fully when you can cast competently.

The basic idea then is to build speed and compression into the rod blank by using as many body muscles as possible and moving it through the correct plane. Modern fast taper rods are designed to store and release a great deal of energy but to do this efficiently they must be used properly. The limited arc of the conventional 'Overhead Thump' used by thousands of anglers just can't do this; the blank is still flexing and therefore absorbing casting effort at the release point. A good technique extends the casting arc considerably so that the blank can be fully flexed before full power is applied. This full compression is known in casting circles as 'locking'; the rod flexes more and more until it finally feels solid. This is one reason why the old slow taper, soft actioned rods were never successful for casting. Their design meant they just bent more and more so you just could not achieve this 'lock-up'.

Once this amount of compression is achieved full body weight and strength can then be channelled into what amounts to a solid lever. Speed is built up quickly and directly transferred into the sinker. At the moment of release the fast recovery of the blank also adds its part to the final sinker speed which by this time will be pretty high. This 'locking' sensation is the hallmark of a good cast giving a far greater distance for effort return than an unlocked blank. It is interesting to note that many of the best tournament distances are made with a feeling of no effort on the part of the caster. Of course effort was applied but because the rod angle was so good and the timing so exact the power was there without

Tournament casters get ultimate distance by good technique and 'hitting' the rod very hard indeed. Just look at the bend in this rod!

strated the need to use the whole body and not just the arms for long casting. When fast taper blanks appeared the limited arc of the layback cast could not compress them properly and therefore the casting action had to be extended. The development work was done by tournament casters, who were obviously most interested in distance and Nigel Forrest, Dennis Darkin and George Brown were well known for their casting performances. Also these men were keen anglers and therefore passed on much of their information so that others could improve their casting range and catch more fish.

The technique itself has several stages from what I would call a 'pendulum layback' to the full blooded 270 degree tournament cast. At each stage the casting arc and drop length are increased giving greater rod speed, compression and therefore ultimate distance potential. Therefore just about every fishing situation can be accommodated from flat open surf beaches where distance may mean everything to restricted rock ledges where a good cast can be difficult to carry out but may still be necessary. The important thing is not to run before you can walk; do not try the full 270 degree tournament cast before you have mastered the basic technique. Start with the simple pendulum layback, a cast that, performed properly, will still send a sinker over 200 yds and gradually progress from there.

Because the arms have a relatively short operating zone the pendulum cast extends this by bringing into use other parts of the body such as the central trunk and the legs. The muscles in these parts also have considerably more power than the arms and therefore by using them all tremendous amounts of energy can be transferred to the rod simply by moving it through the correct plane. Taking this stage by stage you begin with the preliminary swing which tees the sinker up in the correct position for the cast to start. The rod is then drawn down to a level roughly equal to shoulder height which bends the flexible tip portion of the blank. By turning the body at the waist the rod is swept parallel to the ground almost fully compressing the blank's central section, Finally, it is pulled upwards by the arms to get the full body weight and leg muscles behind the rod as it is punched forwards. Done correctly the effort of this last stage should be applied to a fully compressed blank and therefore what amounts to a solid lever so that full sinker speed can be generated. If the cast is not carried out perfectly, and every caster no matter how good will never be perfect all the time, the rod will not quite be locked. However, considerable compression and speed will still have been developed and the sinker will still go a very long way.

For the cast proper please refer to the photographs and captions.

being realised. You seem to be left with the 'If only I'd have hit it harder' feeling yet other efforts which the caster really did feel turn out to give somewhat less than the anticipated result.

Therefore with a less than perfect technique plus a bit of effort it is well within anyone's capability to throw a sinker alone 150 yds. This is the sort of distance that should be attained on most days and over a variety of terrains such as on muddy estuaries, rock platforms and steep shelving beaches. It is not unknown however for quite good tournament casters to fall short on the beach because their technique although powerful is difficult to repeat under fishing conditions. Therefore although I have decided to describe both the 'pendulum' and 'back-cast' styles which are the ones in fashion on the tournament court I personally would say that the pendulum is the best all-round fishing cast. This is especially true with conventional 11 ft 6 inch – 12 ft rods because although longer pendulum rods can and are used they tend to suffer from the same problems as back-casting; lack of manouverability.

Pendulum Casting   This technique has its roots in the 'layback' era when Leslie Moncreiff demon-

Left foot pointing towards 3 o'clock, right foot towards 5 o'clock. Lean away from the casting direction so that body weight is being taken by right leg. Swivel body so that chest faces 6 o'clock. Sinker in front of the rod with about a six foot drop and facing the position from which you wish to start the cast. (See also the plan view sketch). For the beginner I suggest a sinker position of 7 o'clock progressing to 8 o'clock as you get better. The drop length should gradually be increased as you start further round. You should feel comfortable and ready to turn and punch the rod forward.

Send the sinker on the outswing by pushing the rod away with the right hand and lifting the left slightly, sending the sinker towards the 7 o'clock position. The sinker should have enough speed to rise to at least eye level.

As the sinker starts to travel back push down with the left hand and draw the right hand back slowly and slightly to the right. This should swing the sinker back past the right hand side of the rod above your head and above the rod tip. As you feel the sinker pause before starting to fall back, start the cast proper, which must be at exactly this time. The timing is very important and is well worth practising.

Draw the sinker down to the 7 o'clock position, and as the rod comes down bend the legs and start to turn the body. Do not move into the cast too quickly; remember 'slow-in, fast-out'.

With the feet firmly anchored, sweep the rod parallel to the ground, building compression into the central third of the blank and more speed.

Guide the rod towards the casting direction with the arms; body behind and under the rod.

The right arm begins to push strongly in conjunction with the legs and full body weight is transferred to the cast, from the back to the front foot. Body turned to face casting direction; sinker speed increased by punching hard with right arm and pulling the left strongly towards the chest.

The follow-through; rod is angled to give the line a straight and frictionless passage.

PLAN VIEW OF PENDULUM CAST

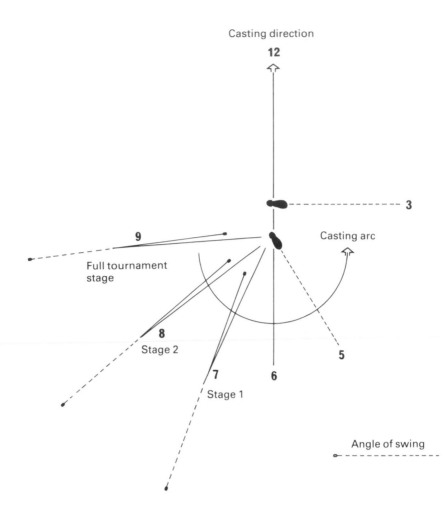

Casting direction

12

3

9

Casting arc

Full tournament
stage

8

Stage 2

5

7

6

Stage 1

Angle of swing

Back-Casting Just as the pendulum cast was developed from the 'layback' the back-cast has its roots in the days of the casting pole. Anglers then used the basic back-to-the-sea stance and pulled the pole up and over the shoulder giving a simple but effective action. The action needed very little alteration to be used with the cane rods and centrepin reels that were next on the scene, then as tackle in general improved so did the distances cast. Just about all the development of this cast was done in East Anglia notably by Fred Williams who coached Dave Dowcra into becoming the first caster to exceed 200 yds with a fixed-spool reel. This in turn led to many anglers using the technique for fishing and for fairly flat open venues it works well.

However for venues with restricted space it is rather limited and many anglers are also put off by the type of rods involved. They would never consider a rod of 13–14 ft long consisting of a 6 ft 1¼ inch butt of either dural or carbon and a one piece 8 ft tip as a fishing rod. Hardly the type of rod to stand and hold in the surf all day, but when the going gets really rough and heavy sinkers around the 8 oz mark are required back-casting is particularly successful. Also the distance between the first ring and the reel position is a long way so that with a fixed-spool reel the coils of line emerging from the spool have a chance to straighten out thereby reducing friction. The point is well shown up in tournaments where back-casters have a very good record of successes. Therefore if you particularly want to use a fixed-spool and fish fairly even, open beaches where the rod spends most of its time in a rod rest then back-casting is worth further consideration. Certainly it does not require quite the co-ordination of movement to get right and beginners usually progress faster than they do with the pendulum cast.

Really the back-cast is only a reversed pendulum because although the body movements are different the rod and sinker follow the same arc. With either cast it is a good idea to study the photographs separately, noting rod and body positions, then string the sequence together using the butt section in your hands. By carrying out these 'dry'

PLAN VIEW OF BACK-CAST

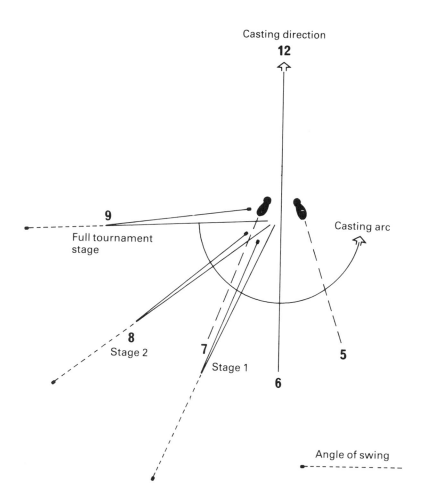

Casting direction

12

Casting arc

9

Full tournament
stage

8
Stage 2

7
Stage 1

6

5

Angle of swing

runs you will be able to feel your body unwinding from the start position through to release and also the way full leg, body and arm strength is applied to the rod during the middle and later stages of the cast. Once you feel that the movement is correct you can tackle up properly and have a go. In the early stages do not try for distance, just cast lazily and smoothly so that you are concentrating mainly on technique. As you feel more confident you can gradually apply more power but not too early in the cast; a good note to follow is 'slow in, fast out' for both techniques. Naturally you will not cast 200 yds straight away and unless you are very keen you probably never will but 140–150 yds should be achieved after a few practice sessions if you are doing things right.

After that you will find that a few regular practice sessions, plus of course some fishing trips, will build distances up to the 175 yd mark with sinker alone; a distance I have already stated as being realistic for most anglers. If things are not going quite as well as expected however do not be put off because as with everything in life you will always

have those ups and downs, so stick at it. Also don't become disolusioned if you seem to stay at one particular distance and just cannot seem to get any further. Usually it's because you are missing a small point so study the photographs again to check and possibly try a few slight alterations to see if that improves matters. Regular practice usually overcomes most problems and I can remember well the period when I could regularly reach 215–218 yds but it seemed that only a superhuman effort would clear 220 yds. Yet by regular practice and a few minor alterations to the cast I achieved 240 yds and then 220 yds represented quite a poor effort!

So stick at it even if progress is not as rapid as you may have hoped. Also look out for details of casting teach-ins or tournaments run by various clubs, magazines and the United Kingdom Surf-casting Federation because these are the perfect places to study technique and get expert advice. Even if you happen to be fishing next to an angler who can obviously cast well never be afraid to wander over and ask for help. Most competent

Stand with back to direction of cast, feet pointing at 5 and 7 o'clock. Twist body to point rod at required angle; 7 o'clock being a good starting place. Drop length about 8 feet to start with, gradually increasing as experience is gained.

Pushing with the left hand, lower the rod tip to send the sinker on the outswing so that it rises to at least eye level.

Bring the sinker back to the right hand side well above the head, and wait for the tension to slacken; this indicates that the cast proper is to start.

At exactly the right time, with the butt cap anchored in the stomach, draw the rod down, bending the legs.

Rod swept parallel to the ground, building up compression in the blank and sinker speed.

Pull strongly with the left arm and push with the legs towards the release point.

The line is released and the sinker flies away.

The follow-through. In most conditions the rod is pointed towards the sinker but with side winds it should be angled so that the line goes straight out.

67

Casting tournaments are an ideal place to watch the top casters in action and to learn.

anglers are only too pleased to assist a keen beginner.

Safety At this point I certainly feel that there is a need to stress the safety aspect of casting. Both the pendulum and the back-cast techniques rely on a very long rod arc to build up speed and compression. During this arc there is a period when the rod is drawn parallel with the ground and at an angle, that should the line break, the sinker would go hurtling along the beach not far off head height. Therefore it is essential that before casting you check that no-one is standing in close proximity on your casting side or in the case of field practice in any area that your sinker could reach. This is one of the major problems for practice because finding a large virtually deserted area that would be suitable is almost impossible in many populated areas.

On flatter beaches the problem does not usually arise because the majority of anglers set-up well back from the waterline thereby leaving a fairly large 'casting zone'. It is the steep venues where problems usually arise because everyone seems intent on getting as near to the sea as possible. This leaves very little safety room at all and therefore you should be very aware of the danger; always make a regular check of leader condition and knots

during the session, use a shorter casting arc so that the majority of power is applied as the rod rises and ask the angler next to you to move back while you cast. You will always get the awkward ones but unless they are complete idiots they will only be too happy to do so. The trouble is that unless they are casters as well they are just not aware of the forces involved and just don't think about it. You therefore have to think for them.

I have seen an angler hit by a flying sinker and luckily for him it was in the back and he was wearing thick clothing that offered some protection. If it had hit him in the head he would have been killed – imagine how you would feel if you had done that. Piers and breakwaters are definite no-go areas for tournament style casts and I get very annoyed with apprentice casters who seem intent on impressing everyone else no matter where they are. A reduced power arc will still get you all the necessary distance without creating an unnecessary danger, so always be careful.

Casting Aids There never has been and probably never will be a device that makes casting easy or compensates for a bad technique. There are however one or two small accessories that can make life a bit easier and overcome some of the

68

many problems that long distance casting brings up.

With multiplier reels the release is a fairly smooth operation but actually gripping a spool full of wet line can be a problem particularly with cold hands. Up to distances of 140 yds with bait you should have no problems if your technique is correct but above this distance slight slipage could occur. It may only be slight but it will still be upsetting and will give a slight reduction in rod compression. On the more serious side it may be enough to let a few turns of the leader off the spool, transmitting full power to the much lighter main line causing it to break.

To avoid this I use a short piece of rubber glove, just long enough to go between the base of the thumb and the first joint. By wrapping the thumb well over the spool, something that most level wind systems make impossible by the way, the rubber is in full contact with the line and grips it very well. By leaving the 'pad' of the thumb clear you can still break the spool lightly should it be necessary. A complete covering would not allow this because the rubber checks the spool in a very snatchy manner and would cause overruns. After considerable experimentation I have found the 'Glovlies' household gloves the best. They are

infact a P.V.C. covering on canvas backing and provide a grippy but quite hard surface. This also allows a cleaner release on the warmer days when the line tends to dry quickly whereas pure rubber tends to 'stick' to dry line making release more difficult.

Breakaway Tackle at Ipswich also market a neat device that fits many popular multipliers even with level winds in situ. A small plastic block with a 'hooked' piece at the bottom clips onto the cross-bar at the back of the reel and on top of the block an oval shaped piece of rubber is hinged. The thumb is placed in the centre of the oval pressing the rubber onto the line; very simple and effective.

A more elaborate device has recently come onto the market produced by Rayner Products of Norwich. Called the Triggerbrake, a name that describes it well, the device consists of a brass plate which hooks onto the front crossbar of the reel cage, then swings right under the spool before turning down to come out beneath the reel. The area where the plating goes under the spool is covered with rubber and it is this part that actually grips the line. The part that comes out below the reel is shaped like a trigger and as the hand holds the rod handle by the reel the index finger hooks around the trigger and pulls back to bring the rubber pad up against the line. Once the cast is complete the finger releases the trigger which allows the pad to move away and release the spool. The device works very well and is quite a work of art to look at as well.

A short length of rubber glove is ideal for additional spool grip.

The Breakaway spool gripping device, the Thumbrake.

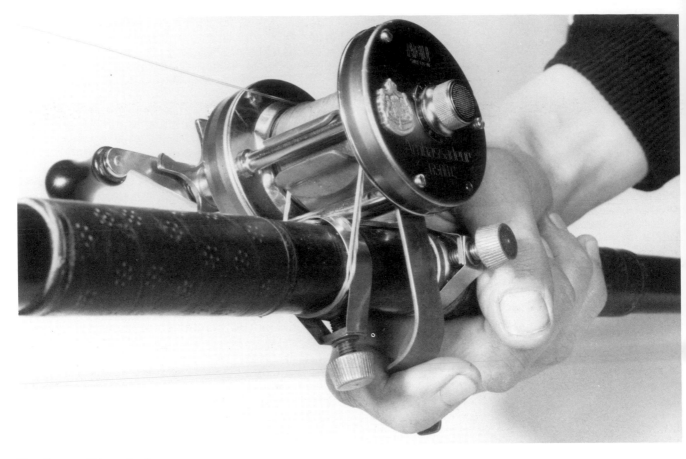

The Rayner Triggerbrake.

With fixed-spools the line is held tightly against the handle by the index finger and as long as the clutch is tightened right up then gripping should not be a problem. However the pressure of hard casting will pull the line tightly across the skin and the snatching of the line on release can make it feel sore. To overcome this it is a good idea to use one of the leather finger protectors sold by chemists to cover wounded fingers. These are very good and are considered essential by tournament casters to avoid stinging. Breakaway Tackle also market a release device for fixed-spools consisting of a small block of plastic that sits on the rod handle directly above the spool. In the centre is a rivet shaped piece that is used to trap the line for casting by holding it down with thumb pressure. To release the line simply take the pressure off and being sprung, the rivet shaped piece lifts up releasing the line. Again a simple but effective device although I prefer the more direct feel of using the index finger.

Baits

I must admit that there are many times during the course of a fishing year when I envy freshwater anglers because as far as bait availability goes they have it made. They can walk into just about any tackle shop and buy enough bait for a day's fishing or alternatively use one of many 'household' products which fit the bill equally as well.

For the sea angler things are more difficult particularly when the fishing is good and therefore the demand for bait high. Unless you happen to live with decent bait beds on your doorstep, an idyllic situation which can easily be spoiled by bad weather, it's a case of planning your trips well in advance and ordering bait at the same time. When the cod are 'in' around my coast a week's notice for lugworm is not enough at times. Even then you have to rely on good conditions because blow lug never last very long even with care, so unless they are used quickly it can be money down the drain.

The problem is that although fish have been taken on all sorts of rubbish over the years and there are areas where artificial luron work well, there is really no alternative to good fresh bait. Match anglers in particular know this. In the cut and thrust of competition where perhaps a hundred or more anglers may be trying to catch the most fish the type, condition and way the bait is presented can make all the difference between a good catch and no fish at all. Many of the really top matchmen move heaven and earth to ensure that they have the best quality bait and plenty of it. Pleasure angling does not require such a dedicated approach but the need for top quality bait is still important. After all the secret of any form of angling is to put the right bait in the right place at the right time. So for the beach angler distance casting can help you to put your tackle in the right place and experience can pick the right time. All that remains then is good bait to complete the chain and hopefully result in a big catch.

Fish often feed on the particular item that is most abundant and easily obtained at the time but it is important to realise that this item can be different depending on the venue, time of year and the weather conditions. Most experienced anglers can tune into these changes knowing that a good storm will bring in quantities of lugworm or shellfish that have been scoured from the bottom, that light onshore winds (particularly if they are easterlies) clear the water and make silver ragworm a good bait and that the crabs have moved inshore to shed their shells making peeler the bait to use. As a general rule you will find that most areas produce fish to one or two specific baits consistently. There will however be other times when another bait is a 'killer' and therefore by learning about a variety of types you will be in a position to use any of them should the need arise.

Lugworm Taking the country as a whole, lugworm must be the most popular and successful all-round bait for sea angling. That may be due in part to its availability, but there is no doubt that just about any fish will take them at some time or another. Certainly on my local East Anglian coastline it is the number one all-round bait and vast beds extend all round the area. The most well known are probably in the salt marshes around the Wash where vast quantities are dug each week for shipment throughout the country. However, even on the open beaches they exist although they are never exposed by even the lowest spring tides at many venues. The fish are usually stuffed to the gills with them after a storm so there is no doubt that they are there.

Basically there seem to be two different types of lugworm; the soft blow lug and the larger and much tougher black lug. Blow lug are not usually found in places that are exposed to the full forces of the open sea but more likely sheltered bays and areas of salt marsh. They tend to be well spread over an area just below the high tide out to and beyond the lowest spring tide mark. Usually it is the smaller worms that inhabit the area at the top of the beach and the size increases as you get towards the area only exposed briefly at the bottom of the tide.

Sand or muddy ground, it doesn't seem to matter because blow lug are found in both although some anglers prefer to use worms dug in clean sand rather than mud. This is because the ground can affect the internal juices of the worm thereby altering its taste but quite honestly I've never really noticed much of a difference in their success. The good thing is whatever the ground blow lug like company and are found in heavily populated patches making digging quite an easy task.

The technique is to pick a place that is heavily covered with the curling, tell-tale, casts and dig a trench just past the area and long enough to encompass them as you dig back. Usually blow lug are within 1½ spits of the surface even in winter so you should not need to go very deep. Then you work back from the trench, over the casts excavating an area which when complete is rectangular in shape. Do not heave the sand out of the hole just turn it over backfilling the trench you have just dug. This makes the job much easier and doesn't leave the beach looking like a bomb site or in a hazardous condition for bathers if it is summer. If the area is a bit wet you may have to dig a trench down two sides of the rectangle to drain the water out of the sand. Wet, sloppy sands make spotting the worms quite difficult.

Black lug on the other hand are often found in the hard sand of the exposed beach and the reason that they survive is that they burrow much deeper than blow lug, often three feet or more. Even so in really rough weather they are sucked from their burrows and washed inshore and at these times it is possible to collect quite a few just walking along the tideline.

With blow lug in their shallow U-shaped burrow a flat tinned potato fork is the best tool to dig them with but the deep straight burrow of the black lug really has to be tackled with a small bladed, purpose built spade. Because they are usually well spaced you will be digging for individual worms anyway and the technique is quite specialised requiring considerable practice to perfect. The idea is to dig a small hole following the burrow of the worm as you go. As long as you keep it free from sand you should eventually spot the tail of the worm. Now is the time to get going because black lug can disappear at a fair rate of knots especially if you cut the tail. As soon as you expose a fleshy part of the worm grab it and then by loosening the sand around it you should be able to pull it out. Freed from the burrow the blow lug usually spew their guts out which allows them to be kept for a longer period in paper. If you want to tank them you have to quickly pop them into a bucket of sea water but even so some will still burst.

For those of you who can't or do not want to dig your own lugworm most coastal tackle shops have daily deliveries. However as I said earlier you will probably have to order them well in advance, to ensure a supply. I buy mine from a reliable digger due to the cost and effort advantage and really they are as good as I could get anyway. Some shops supply absolute rubbish, small soft worms that split at the sight of a hook and therefore it is well worth trying a few different places until you find a dealer who is reliable and supplies good worms. Having done that however be sure to do your part by always turning up to collect your bait.

Storing lugworm is always a problem but there are several ways of tackling it. Blow lug are very soft and watery when they are first dug and require drying out on old newspaper before use. This process toughens the skins slightly, giving the worms a greater resistance to the whiplash of hard casting and helps them to last longer. The 'dailies' that use the cheaper paper seem to be best because they absorb the moisture better and by

keeping the worms in a refrigerator with regular paper changes they should keep for three days with only minimal losses. You can sometimes keep them longer especially if it was cold when they were dug but the losses get more severe until about six days when those that are left have become very small and dried out.

For dry storage black lug should be gutted and laid individually on newspaper to dry out. Although they also shrink considerably their large initial size means that they still make a fair size bait by themselves. After a few hours they become long and thin resembling sticks of liquorice in both looks and texture. This process toughens them up considerably and coupled with the thickness of the skin makes it virtually impossible to cast them off the hook. Rolled up in newspaper black lug can last a week in a fridge and even after that as they go 'off' they are still useable, unlike the gooey mess of blow lug. In fact in this 'high' state they can prove very successful particularly for dabs.

For storage exceeding a week one method is to put the worms in salt water tanks. Most anglers have probably read about 'tanking' in the monthly magazines and it has proved popular with some anglers and less so with others. Both blow and black lug can be kept in tanks but it is very important to keep the water at a cool, even temperature, and examine regularly for dead worms. If you leave them they will contaminate and kill the rest in no time at all. Experience has shown that blow lug, being a watery worm to begin with become even more watery if tanked and there is no doubt that their fish catching ability is reduced. They are all right with lots of fish about but tend to get washed off the hook very quickly because most of the sand which helps hold them together has been cleared through their bodies. Black lug are better because their tough skin holds them onto the hook and results seem to be much better. Quite honestly I wouldn't bother to tank blow lug at all.

Freezing is another method that can be used. With blow lug I find the best way is to gut them as you would black lug and let them dry out fully on newspaper. Then mount them onto a hook with a short snood and freeze the lot. Naturally they really do shrink and you need quite a few to make a decent bait but this is a good way of keeping left over bait. After a few trips you will probably have enough for a complete session. When you decide to go, transport the completed snoods in a food vacuum flask and only take out each one as it is required for use. That way, they stay frozen for several hours. Black lug can be treated in the same manner and I can assure you that both types of worm catch fish very well. The only point to remember is that they do soften quickly as they thaw out in the water and are not as resistant to crabs etc, as say a fresh worm. Be sure therefore to rebait more frequently than you do normally.

Ragworm This species of worm is not quite as popular as lugworm, probably because it tends to be more expensive, but tends to be more 'meaty' and therefore more resistant to the attacks of crabs. Basically there are three main types of ragworm that interest the angler. These are 'king' or 'red' ragworm, 'white' or 'silver' ragworm and 'harbour' ragworm. All three catch fish but usually each species is aimed at a particular species of fish in a particular area.

King rag are probably the best known and are by far the largest; worms in excess of two feet are not uncommon. More often however the worms are in the eight to twelve inch bracket and this is the size that most professional diggers supply. The trouble with digging them is that they tend to be more scattered than lugworm, not as individual as black lug but not as close as blow lugworm. Usually trenching is still the way to get them but you have to turn over a lot of ground to get the worms. If they are really scattered then you can sometimes locate them by walking slowly over the ground looking for a spurt of water sent out by the worm as the ground is compressed.

The type of ground king rag tend to favour can also make digging for them difficult. Usually it is areas of that smelly black mud mixed with shingle or shells. Estuaries and harbours often have this sort of ground although on more exposed coasts banks of mussel beds are also worth exploring. To dig successfully you must use a fork and even this isn't easy. The thick oozing mud can be difficult by itself let alone when mixed with stones and ragworm have the habit of disappearing down their burrow at lightning speed. Also they can break their bodies very easily when in trouble so it is quite easy to end up with lots of pieces rather than whole worms.

Once dug, king rag can be kept for five to seven days by storing in trays and covering with damp seaweed. Be sure to change or re-dampen the weed every couple of days or so. You can also wrap them singly in newspaper as with black lug and this certainly toughens the skins well although I find that they don't seem to last quite as long. With both of these methods temperature is obviously important and a fridge is really the only way to maintain a cool but even level.

Longer term storage is also easy because king rag keep very well indeed in aerated, salt water tanks. Although they also become a bit washed out and more watery than when first dug the meaty nature of their body ensures that they still remain a good bait. It is also better to keep two to three inches of shingle in the bottom of the tank so that the worms burrow in and keep separated. If they are placed just in water they tend to bunch up and start cutting each other to pieces with the very efficient set of pincers that their mouths are equipped with. You will lose a few worms anyway because king rag are cannabalistic, making short work of a companion if they get a bit hungry.

White or silver ragworm are a species that have built up a fantastic reputation for success over the past few years particularly amongst matchmen. As their name suggests they are white in appearance with a silver hue down the centre of their backs. In fact there is speculation that white and silver ragworm are two different species but from an angling viewpoint they can be treated as the same.

As I have said their reputation as a fish catcher is second to none and some matchmen would sell their souls for a reliable supply of white rag. Personally I feel that they are overrated in many instances because although there are certainly times when the fish will not look at anything else, at many other times the local favourite will fish better. As a generalisation white rag seem to work best in clear water conditions. On the south coast of England and over rocky ground where the water can be fairly clear white rag are excellent but on the east coast where the water tends to be murky with suspended sand and silt particles they are often out fished by good blood filled lugworm. The clear water theory is backed up here by the fact that white rag fish very well when their is a period of high pressure giving clear skies and light onshore winds. In these conditions the sand and silt particles tend to settle on the bottom increasing visibility considerably. The thing is that for match angling you just can't take the chance that conditions will not be like this so a supply of white rag is a must.

White ragworm are often hard to obtain. They

Silver rag – a bait that can be 'deadly' at times but also much overrated on many other occasions.

73

certainly are not obtainable through tackle shops but there are now a few professional diggers who will supply them. The only way really is to dig them yourself and from what I have learnt from anglers in other parts of the country there seems to be some in most areas. The size available probably varies however because in most areas where lugworm is dug in fairly clean sand you will find the small white rag which make a good bait for pout, whiting and flounders. Larger white rag, or 'snakes' as they are often called, tend to inhabit fairly small areas which is one of the reasons that those anglers who know where they are tend to keep it quiet.

Favoured areas usually tend to be where clean sand is mixed with light shingle or small shells and also where there are banks of tube worms. These are easily spotted because their cases poke out of the sand an inch or so giving a 'bristly' appearance to the ground. Unfortunately they do not give themselves away by casts so at first you have to explore the area to find out their location. Luckily they tend to keep very close to the surface, often two inches and not usually more than six to seven inches even in winter. Trenching is again the method using a fork to avoid cutting too many worms and the very best worms are often only dug on the very lowest spring tides. This is the time when the tide goes out furtherest and in many areas is the only time the white rag can be dug.

Naturally, if you can only dig on these tides which occur only twice a month storing the worms is very important. Luckily they keep extremely well in tanks, probably better than any other species of worm in fact. Once you have lifted the worm from the sand place it immediately in a bucket of sea water. When you get home sort out the worms removing all cut and damaged worms for use as soon as possible otherwise they will contaminate the others as they die. All the good worms can be put into their containers and here it pays to take care not to overcrowd them. I prefer to keep 20–40 worms in a number of small containers rather than 200 in one. That way it is easier to keep an eye on their condition and if tragedy strikes there are a lot less worms to loose.

Surprisingly it is not essential to aerate the water and I have found that the worms keep better without aeration as long as you change it once a week or sooner if the water starts to go cloudy. If you cannot do this then you will have to use a pump and airstone to oxygenate the water but be careful not to overdo it. Set the valve to give only a trickle of bubbles from the airstone because too much oxygen in the water causes the worms to bubble along the backs and die. Make sure when you collect the fresh water that it is from the open sea and that you bring it down to the existing temperature of the container before you change the worms.

Some people also like to put some shingle or coral sand in the bottom of the container for the worms to bury themselves in but I have not found this necessary and in fact it is easier to keep an eye on their condition without. The only time I use it is when taking the worms on a long journey because it stops them from getting thrown about in the bottom of the container. White rag keep very well and as long as the temperature is low and the water clean they last two to three months with only the minimum of losses and without a noticeable food source.

Harbour rag are the smallest and least used of the three species of ragworm. From a distance casting aspect they are a bit of a non-starter because their delicate nature rules out forceful style. Mind you, harbour rag are really used for species such as flounders which are normally close in anyway so the casting aspect doesn't enter into the picture.

As their name suggests they prefer the muddy grounds of harbours and estuaries and are found in densely populated patches. The messier and smellier the mud the better they like it although it should have a reasonably firm, clay-like texture. Usually estuaries are favourite and the worms extend well inland when the water becomes blackish. Digging is not too difficult and the best way is to lift out a clod of mud then break it apart with your hands, pulling out the ragworm as you find them. Don't pull too hard because they break very easily.

You can keep them alive in salt water in a similar manner to the other ragworm but it hardly seems worth the trouble. I normally dig them the day before they are required and lay them out on dry newspaper overnight. This drains off the excess moisture and toughens them up a bit so that they stay on the hook as well as possible.

Crab Apart from being bait stealing pests for most of the time crabs make an excellent bait and there are not many species of fish that will swim past them. At times crabs can be deadly; often when the first crabs move inshore and peel at the beginning of spring and annually is responsible for many good catches and specimen fish. It is a bait that along with silver rag has built up a tremendous reputation with match anglers as a fish catcher and at one time it was believed to be so good that many organisers actually banned it. It is also a bait that has an air of mystique about it and many anglers actually shy away from using it. Why, I don't know because it is just another bait to be used at times and in places when it is likely to work best. As long as you follow a few simple points you shouldn't have any trouble.

As far as the angler is concerned the only time that crabs are useful as a bait is when they are in the process of shedding their shells (peelers) or have actually done it (softbacks). As with all the other members of the crustacean family which have this hard outer shell crabs have to shed this shell at various stages during their growth. As they get larger they obviously get too big for their shell and therefore it has to be got rid of. This is done by the crab passing a quantity of calcium into its existing body shell which gradually breaks it down causing it to become very brittle. Having done this the crab absorbs water into its body so that it begins to swell. This swelling pressurises the shell and causes it to split so that the crab can then push it off. Underneath this old shell the crab has been growing a new one but at this stage it is only like a tough skin. Having pushed off the old shell the crab continues to expand pushing the new shell out. Then over a period of a few days the new shell hardens to the normal level and the crab pushes out most of the water it has absorbed. The body returns to its normal size leaving a shell which is really oversize. However the crab obviously continues to grow until it fills the shell, when the process starts over again.

It is during this soft stage that the crab is most vulnerable to attack from fish and therefore once it senses that the process has started it hides away under rocks, breakwaters, weed or anything else that offers shelter. It is also interesting to note that the female crab has to be soft for mating to take place and many anglers feel that the female crabs make a better bait. This is due to the fact that the females must put out a scent for the male crab to find them and therefore the fish probably can as well. Mind you one has only to cut any crab, male or female, in half when it is in the peeling stage to see the oozing orange juices which are going to attract fish. The only point I would make is that crabs are at their very best as a bait when they are just about to shrug off the old shell because it is at this point that you can remove every piece of shell easily and the new body is at its most juicy stage. Peelers that are not far into the moulting process can be quite difficult to peel properly and I tend to use them whole for cod and bass at this stage. As long as the back shell is removed they seem to work just as well. Once the shell gets slightly crisp the crabs don't seem very good and you usually find the inside is very watery and lacking in juices when you cut them in half. I would think that the fish like them but they just do not have the 'pulling power' of a fresh moulting crab.

The first crabs move inshore to peel as the water warms up at the beginning of spring and during late May and early June they are moulting in mass. This is the time when they are easiest to find and some of the experienced crabbers can pick hundreds in a single tide. Due to its liking of cover you want to look in areas of rock, under groynes, dykes in saltmarshes, the bottom of harbour walls, under wreckage or in fact anything that may offer cover. Ideally the covering object should be on sand or

mud so that the crab can bury itself so don't just look but scrape through the sand with your fingers. Some people hate putting their hands into dark murky places and therefore use some sort of rake but take it easy because it is very easy to damage them.

Soft crabs are easily recognised and they just do not have the energy to run away once uncovered. Peelers on the other hand are a bit more difficult but with practice it becomes easy. Usually they are less aggressive than the normal crab, tending to back away when uncovered rather than adopting the 'claws-up attack' position. Not always of course, so it pays to check each one. This is done by breaking away the last segment of the leg and drawing it away gently. If it leaves a white piece of gristle then it is not a peeler but if it reveals a soft fleshy leg segment then it is a peeler. Hen crabs are usually carried underneath the male when they are peeling which makes identification easy. Separating them is another matter because the male isn't usually too keen to give up his conquest! The only other way if you don't fancy collecting your own is to buy them and in fact this is the only way in winter when the crabs move offshore. At this time some shops buy them from Devon and Cornwall where the milder air temperature and warmer Gulf Stream seas allow crabs to be collected all the year round. The only problem then is the price because they are not cheap.

Crabs can be kept quite well in a box covered in wet seaweed as long as you keep them cool. This slows down the peeling process because once peeling actually starts the crabs quickly die without an adequate supply of water. If you keep them in water for long periods they will peel and harden and therefore if you don't use them they will be useless. Many of the top anglers keep their crabs in fridges using a system of trays to grade them. Those that are furthest from peeling go in at the bottom, then as they move nearer to peeling they move to the next shelf. The top shelf is for crabs that are on the verge of peeling and therefore in peak condition for bait. The crabs can be brought on by taking them out of the fridge and placing in salt water. This allows them to take in more water and more forward in the peeling process. Unless the crabs are crawling out of their shells you should be able to keep them for a week easily with regular changes of seaweed.

Alternatively you can freeze them although there are various opinions on their effectiveness. Some people prefer to freeze them whole, others like to peel them first and some use quick freezing solutions based on glycerol to avoid tissue breakdown. Personally I dislike using anything that can add an unnatural taint to the bait. I have had the best results with frozen crab by peeling them completely then mounting on the hook and freezing the lot. The crabs are then transported in a food flask as with frozen lug so that they are still frozen when cast out. This I feel is much better because both crab and lug seem to go 'off' very quickly once they thaw out and seem to be far less effective.

Also before leaving this section on crabs I would like to mention the humble hermit. This crab goes about living in discarded whelk shells and as soon as it gets too small it is changed for a bigger one. Therefore the head, legs and claws are covered with its own shell but the main part of the body is always soft and makes an excellent bait. Cod, thornback ray and smoothhound are particularly partial to a hermit crab but the problem for the angler is getting them and keeping them. The best bet is where whelk boats operate because they get hundreds and just toss them aside. The trouble is that they must be used immediately or frozen because once out of water they die very quickly. Hermit is a very neglected bait but if you do get hold of some be sure to use them because they really work well.

Shellfish Just about every species of shellfish that inhabits our coastline can be pressed into service as a bait although its effectiveness tends to vary considerably from area to area. Overall I wouldn't say that they are as effective as worms or crab but there are times, particularly after severe onshore gales that they can give quite spectacular results. Rocky areas are more usually associated with shell fish but razorfish, cockles and butterfish all inhabit sandy ground so it is a bait worth considering for all types of venue.

Mussels are probably the most well known of all the shellfish and inhabit areas of rock, harbours, groynes and the piles of most piers. It is therefore quite an easy bait to collect although you may find some difficulty in locating areas of really large mussels in the southern half of the country. In the north however mussel is far more abundant and is considered an excellent bait for most species of fish but especially cod and coalfish. The only real problem is keeping it on the hook and straight from the shell it is a bait that is very soft and 'wet' and exceptionally difficult to cast distances over 70 yards. Laying them out on newspaper helps because it draws out some of the moisture and some anglers sprinkle a little salt over them to toughen the flesh further. Then it's a case of putting plenty on the hook, wrapping with elasticated thread and casting as smoothly as possible.

Razorfish is another fairly well known bait which inhabits sandy ground living down a burrow between a foot and three feet below the surface. During periods of rough weather they can be collected from the beach as the strong swells suck them from their homes and wash them ashore. Normally they inhabit the spring low tide marks and therefore you will have to wait until the water recedes as far back as possible. Collection can be

done by several methods, including straight-forward digging with a fork although this is rather slow and reduces the number collected before the tide begins to make. Large razors can be extracted from their holes using a specially designed spear but again it is a technique that requires practice before you can collect large numbers. The easiest way is to slowly walk over the sand looking for the tell-tale key-hole shaped entrance to its burrow and the squirt of water as the ground is disturbed. Once located simply pour some salt down the hole and wait for the razorfish to surface. This takes only a few moments but be sure to let the razor fish shell emerge as well; don't just grab at the feeding syphon which emerges first because it will break off. Once you see the shell take hold and pull firmly but steadily to loosen the hold of the muscular foot at the bottom end of the shell. Having collected them you can keep them alive for about a week in a fridge but the only long term storage solution is to freeze them. This is done quite simply by blanching first with boiling water and then popping them in the freezer in bags of about ten. Although they are not quite as good as when fresh they still catch fish and are a handy substitute if your more usual bait is not available.

Other smaller shellfish such as butterfish, cockles, slipper limpets, clams, whelks and piddock clams can really all be dealt with together. Apart from clams which can be quite large the others are all fairly small shellfish which inhabit a variety of areas and if you happen to live near one of them then they could prove a successful bait. I must admit that my own fishing experience has been very limited with these last mentioned baits yet other anglers say that they can be successful for specific species in very specific areas but as a general rule worm baits and crab prove much better.

One addition that does not get much attention is the humble shrimp or prawn. This extremely common shellfish is found in the stomach of just about everything that swims near a sandy shore line and the cod and whiting in my area are usully stuffed to the gills with them. They are easily collected with a small trail or push net and can be kept alive in an areated bucket of salt water for a few hours. As a bait they can be effective for many species even though their scent value is low, and the only problem is casting distance. They are fairly fragile and do not tolerate excessive casting stresses. Prawns are much bigger and make good baits for mid-water fish such as bass and pollack, when floatfished.

Fish Baits To most anglers fish baits mean mackerel and herring and they are certainly the most used. Both mackerel and herring are medium size mid-water fish that shoal in massive numbers – at least they did before they were overfished by commercial fleets – and they form a basic food source for many species. Most of the really big predators feed exclusively on fish and a whole mackerel or herring makes an excellent bait when fished from a boat. There are a few shore locations where such large fish can be found but these are fairly rare and in general the beach angler is more concerned with smaller sections of the fish or with their smaller cousins sprats and whitebait.

The priority with fish is absolute freshness – if at all possible and this will ential catching them yourself for immediate use or at the very least getting them direct from the inshore boats for freezing. The difference between a fresh or fresh frozen fish and shop bought fish is amazing in both looks, texture and effectiveness. Mackerel or herrings straight from the sea have a beautiful clean skin that seem to reflect all the colours of the rainbow. Cut into the body and they just ooze blood and juices and the flesh is much firmer, quite rubbery in fact. Compare this to the dull, dry appearance of a shop bought fish whose flesh seems to just flake away from the skin and you will soon see why the guy with fresh bait catches consistently while those with shop bought fish only get the odd one or two. With scavengers like whiting the difference isn't always so marked but try it with a species like thornback ray and you will soon see the importance of ultra-fresh fish bait.

Both mackerel and herring seem to be equally as effective and really I think it's the angler who seems to be the one with a preference if anyone has one. Possibly the skin of the mackerel is that bit tougher and helps the bait to stay on the hook but in general I am quite happy using either species. Sprats and whitebait are also very good being very similar to herring and can be used in sections or whole. The convenient thing is that fish freezes very well, particularly the blast frozen stuff, and seems to remain in excellent condition for about three months. After that it does seem to slowly deteriorate although its value as a bait is still good.

Sandeel is another excellent fish bait and is used intensively in the south west of the country for bass and rays. It is however very good for many other species of fish when used either whole or in sections. There are two types of sandeel, the greater and the lesser, with the former growing to lengths of over a foot. The lesser is the one more commonly used for bait being about 6 inches long and can be fished either live or dead. As with prawns they will not survive heavy casting and therefore fished live they are a short range bait only. As a dead bait they can be secured better and can be cast to maximum range just as successfully as a bunch of worms.

The normal way of obtaining sandeels is to buy them frozen and this should not prove difficult as many dealers stock them. I would however inspect them before purchasing to check their general condition. Being a fish they should still look in good condition if they were frozen quickly after capture; a dull appearance is a sure sign that they were left a while. The best again are the eels that have been blast frozen because they are frozen very quickly and therefore are in very good condition. If you happen to live in an area where they are quite common you may like to collect them yourself. In the estuaries of rivers such as the Teign in Devon they shoal up in large numbers and can be netted although a net is an expensive item and really only for the professional. However as the tide drops sandeels bury themselves in the sand and can be collected individually.

The method for doing this is to use an old knife that has been cut to form a hook at the bottom. Known as a vingler, it is pushed into the sand and drawn through it in a sort of figure of eight pattern. Once the blade comes up against some resistance the vingler is slowly withdrawn until the hooked section catches the eel's body and pulls it out of the sand. As the eel emerges you must use the other hand to trap it otherwise it will be back in like greased lightning! Another tip is to wear a rubber glove because the sand also hides weaver fish and the sting from them is highly poisonous. Collecting sandeels is quite good fun and if you don't have a knife you can run the heel of your boot through the sand which should dislodge a few. They squirm on the surface for only a few seconds so you have to be quick otherwise they bury themselves again. As with many types of bait collecting low water springs are the best time for quantity and quality.

Another fish bait that can be used is squid. I find that it is more consistently successful when used from a boat than the shore but even then it tends to blow hot and cold. Most of the squid in home waters that are caught commercially are pretty big, around 4–5 lb in weight and therefore have to be cut up for bait. Not that this is a problem but whole squid or the head and tentacles can make a good bait for larger species. Therefore I prefer the Californian 'Calumari' squid that are imported in deep frozen blocks and are available from many fishmongers. Being around 4 to 6 inches in length they are ideal to use whole although distance casting is not practical with this size of bait. If you need to get well out then use strips or a few tentacles which are very tough and rubbery and stay on the hook exceptionally well. In my area this can work for thornback ray quite well but generally this bait performs poorly. The addition of a couple of lug to make a cocktail seems much better and therefore it can be handy to make a packet of lug last a bit longer. In other parts of the country it seems to work a lot better particularly for conger and large bass so it could be worth a try.

Fishing Techniques

In the previous chapters I have discussed all the individual items and skills that the competent shore angler requires but now I want to turn my attention to probably the most important part – the time when they are put to use. The best rod and reel, bait and casting ability do not guarantee a good catch. The way you use them, the times you fish and how you actually fish have a greater bearing on what you finally end up with. As the saying goes, good tools do not automatically make a good craftsman.

Fish Location As with all aspects of angling fish location must rate as the most important single aspect. Even the best anglers cannot perform the impossible, which is to catch fish when there aren't any in front of them. A good example is match fishing where you fish from pegged positions. Really competent anglers can go fishless while others only yards away, steadily catch fish and no matter how hard they try they just cannot get anything. The pleasure angler of course is not limited to fishing in a certain place unless the beach is absolutely packed out and therefore should choose his spot carefully to give the best chance of success.

Fish lead very complex lives; their moods, feeding habits and food supplies are constantly changing depending on the time of year, weather conditions and the state of the tidal flow. At any one time the fish could be at any of a number of locations feeding well or not at all and what you have to do as an angler is try your best to tune into these changing features, analyse them and then try to put

Get the time, place and conditions right and you may catch a really big fish like this 20¼lb North Norfolk cod.

78

yourself in the best possible position to catch the fish. I don't think it is coincidence that many really good anglers live on or very close to the coast. Not only do they have the opportunity to fish at a moment's notice but they seem to have a 'feel' for the fish and the way the conditions affect them. No matter what the tide, or weather may be doing they always seem to know the best areas to go and try. By doing this the 'luck' element, which is always a factor in fishing, is reduced to a minimum.

Naturally different species have different preferences and no two locations are the same. However you will soon discover the species that frequent your coast and these will be the ones to concentrate on. Around Norfolk and Suffolk where I fish we are mainly concerned with cod, whiting and flatfish with the possibility of a few bass or even thornback ray. Every season these fish follow a migratory pattern moving inshore and offshore depending on the time of year and to a lesser extent the weather. However this latter point only alters the movement by a few weeks or so. Using cod as a specific example they first show on the beaches in Southern Suffolk in the middle of October when they are mixed in with large shoals of whiting. By the end of October and first week in November they have moved up to Great Yarmouth. As November progresses they move round the Norfolk coast until December when they are present on all venues. After Christmas the fish above about 5 lb begin to move offshore to spawn and January and early February are very poor. Then by the last week in February or first week in March the spring run begins and usually continues until the end of April or even early May when the last few finally move away.

Migratory movements similar to this but obviously at varying times of the year are followed by most species and are fairly predictable. Once you know that the fish are moving inshore in your area the next question is to reduce the choice to a much more limited area; in a specific length of beach. The fish seem to move into very specific areas and then stay there for periods sometimes as short as a week and sometimes as long as a complete season. The strange thing with this is that although there are always beaches that are fairly consistent the fact that the beach fishes well one day is no guarantee that it will the next. The availability of food is obviously an important factor as are weather conditions which may have roughed up the sea and changed the contours of the bottom. Whatever the reason it is relatively unimportant as long as you find out so that you are at the right beach at the right time.

Again if you live on the coast you will have first hand information when and where the fish are in but for the angler who lives inland other sources of information have to be found. You could study the reports in the angling press but due to unavoidable delays in the report being received and finally printed they are out of date by at least a week. That could leave you fishing for fish that have already been caught or have moved away. A better bet is your local press if they have a fishing page because their reports were probably received within a couple of preceding days and are more likely to be up to date. Another way is to visit the local tackle shop because with its steady turnover of anglers information is likely to be as up to date as possible even if somewhat exaggerated by one or two. The best way of all is to build up a number of friends who live on the coast and know exactly what is being caught. This way an angling 'grapevine' builds up with information constantly being exchanged and it is information which is about as up to date as you can get. Whichever method you use will depend on where you live and who you know but at least you can get a general idea on the beaches fishing well and that is a start.

Having set your mind on a beach the next thing is to decide when to fish it and where the fish are likely to be concentrated in the largest numbers. Several factors will affect this; the state of the tide, the contours of the beach, and naturally, weather conditions. Hit all three just right and you are likely to make a good catch but get them all wrong and you are wasting your time. Usually it is a case of doing your best to get the biggest percentage right and at least catch a few fish. Let us now consider each point separately to simplify the situation as much as possible.

1. State of Tide There is no doubt that some beaches tend to fish much better at a particular state of tide; either flood or ebb. In many areas not only does the tide move in an out but there is a general flow along the beach the direction of which reverses as the tide changes. The distance the tide moves in and out and the strength of the flow varies with the gravitational pull of the sun and the moon. Basically when they are positioned in line their gravitational effects work together and you get the strongest flows and the highest tide (Spring tides) and when the moon is at its quarter the flow is relatively weak and the tides are several feet lower in height (Neap tides). Out of the two states the Springs seem to be the most successful, moving the fish inshore and increasing the time that they seem to be willing to feed, particularly during periods of prolonged calm seas.

Fish are stimulated into feeding by the tidal flow but it appears that there is a certain water speed that they feed best. In my area cod and whiting are caught in most numbers about an hour after the tide has reached its mid point; two hours before high water or before low water. This seems to be the peak time and sometimes you can almost set your watch by them. Sometimes when they are really feeding well you can catch them at any time

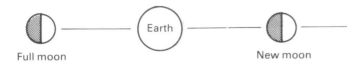

Full moon   Earth   New moon   Sun

Spring tides occur when sun and moon are attracting in the same line

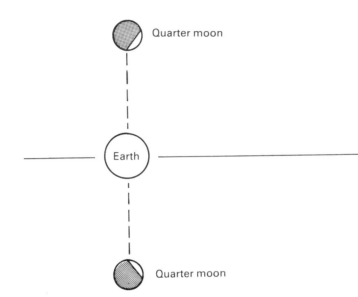

Quarter moon

Earth   Sun

Quarter moon

Neap tides occur when sun and moon act against each other

although this is rare and generally the two hour rule applies. Slack water is generally pretty useless except with flatfish which move out of the sand and actively hunt for food rather than letting the tide bring it to them.

Slack water does not always occur at high and low tide; sometimes it is when the water is actually moving in or out. Around Gt. Yarmouth the tide direction does change at high and low water and the two hour before rule applies. At Mundesley on the North Norfolk Coast however the direction changes at about two hours after high and low water. Therefore although the two hour rule still applies in flow terms it actually occurs at high and low water respectively and true to form this is when they fish best.

This lateral flow along the coast can also affect the way the beach fishes due to its geographical position on the coastline. If you take a look at an Ordnance Survey map of your area you can see the bays, headlands or even slight alterations that could cause food to collect in certain areas when the tide direction is a certain way. The only real way to find out is either to try and question some of the local anglers or fish the beach yourself at varying states of the tide. Personally I like to fish a beach myself because whilst local information is often accurate it can also be limited to the casting range of the anglers fishing. One or two venues in my area are generally reckoned to be best on the last two hours of the ebb and over low water. This is because a large gulley runs parallel with the shoreline at a range of about 100 yds from the low tide mark and most anglers can reach it. At high water however a cast of 150–170 yds can be needed and therefore it is only the better casters who even bother to fish at this time. With more fish moving in at this time they often make a real killing yet virtually have the beach to themselves. As a general rule you will find that shallow beaches are better on the flood tide whilst venues which offer fairly deep water will fish on either tide.

2. *Contours of the Beach* Areas where the tide moves in and out over a considerable distance enable the angler to have a really clear view of the ground he wishes to fish. Gullies, banks and patches of rock and weed are all visible so that you can pick the area that looks best. Basically the gullies are usually the favourites because they act as traps for any food washing about the bottom and also the fish seem to move along them like cars on a road. Therefore if your bait can consistently be placed there fish should always come across it. Patches of rough ground are also worth investigation especially where they are positioned in areas which are otherwise clear. Again they act as collection points for food that is being washed about over the bottom plus of course the crabs and shellfish that live there. In some areas the contours are not easily identifiable, appearing totally flat but closer inspection should still reveal very slight depressions of only a few inches plus patches of gravel here and there. Believe it or not even these small differences can cause an accumulation of food and therefore an accumulation of fish.

In other areas the tide does not move in and out very far and the angler does not have the chance to see the ground he wants to fish. At first the beach may appear a constant stretch of featureless sand and shingle but by careful observation and a degree of patience the better spots can be found. One of the easiest ways is to learn by observation. In other words watch other anglers and try to keep a note of where the better catches come from.

Open matches are good for this because once a few have been fished a pattern soon developes. Mind you, you also have to consider the calibre of the angler fishing because if you see someone catching consistently at a range of 80 yds it is hopeless going along and blasting out 150 yds or falling short. Obviously there is a fish attracting feature there but you have got to try and place your bait near it.

Another way is to watch the way the tide flows along the beach although this is really only possible in calm weather. Changes in depth can be signalled by slight turbulence or eddying of the surface water and anything that is different can be worth trying. In really rough weather the breaking waves often show the contours of the bottom quite well by surfing where there are banks and shallow areas and remaining reasonably calm where the water is deeper. The shallower the water the easier these features show up so the best time to have a look is at low tide when the water has gone out the furthest. Although most anglers seem to rush for the deeper parts you may find that there are certain times when the fish prefer the shallows particularly if they are home to lugworms. Several beaches I know fish better if you cast onto the bank when the water is calm because the fish actively hunt for lugworm. When it's rough they stay where it's a bit deeper waiting for the worms to be washed to them.

3. *Weather Conditions* These are probably the most important single factor out of the three mentioned because fish are very sensitive to changes in atmospheric pressure. Warm and cold fronts moving across the country seem to switch fish on and off like a light bulb and somehow they seem to

Areas where the tide moves over a fair distance are ideal to pick out fish holding areas such as gullies and rocks.

know that bad weather is on its way hours or even days before it actually arrives. The best spot on the best beach on the best tide can prove useless if the weather conditions are not right and unfortunately although you can do quite a bit to get the others right it is pure chance with the weather.

You can go fishing on two consecutive days with the conditions seemingly identical but the fish feed well one day yet are gone the next. Therefore it is virtually impossible to generalise on what constitutes the best conditions for fishing particularly when different species seem to have different preferences. With cod in my area you usually find that during periods of high pressure with light winds and clear skies they stay offshore during daylight but move inshore under the cover of darkness. In periods of low pressure the water tends to colour up more even if the sea is calm and with overcast skies during the day the fishing can often be as good as it is at night. Naturally there are always those occasions that prove you wrong and I have taken several excellent hauls when the bright sunlight has made a trip almost summerish in mid-December.

Periods of rough weather can also have an effect on the quality of fishing because apart from stirring up quantities of food they can also alter the characteristics of the beach. All those hot spots suddenly have to be replotted. Really though it is the food that interests the fish and as soon as the water calms down enough they are in for a spree. One or two tides after the storm are usually thought of as the best times but much depends on how severe it has been. Small blows which last only a day or a few days usually perks the fishing up no end and in these circumstances I like to move in as soon as conditions start to settle if possible. Really bad storms which go on for a week or even more and produce those mountainous seas that tear the beaches apart and rip up the weed from the sea bed are better left for a few days before you go. Immediately after the blow the sea is so full of floating weed that it can be virtually impossible to fish anyway. Of course if the beach is fishable it is well worth a try while the blow is on and I have taken many good catches at such times. One of the benefits on being able to cast well is that you can cast above average distances even in a head wind and clear the surf nicely.

Study the area to be fished and search out the beaches where the fish are being caught. Pick the right tide for that beach and the spot that you feel should produce and finally keep an eye on the weather for the few days before you go because although you cannot control it you may find that particular parts of your coastline are affected by winds in different ways and that could influence your final choice of venue.

Baiting-up From a distance casting point of view

this means keeping your bait on the hook successfully so it arrives on the sea bed in as good a condition as possible. When fishing at closer range you can start to worry about presentation because for some species it can make a difference. However as the majority of fish feed by smell then I think that as long as it smells right they will take it and they are not going to be able to do this if all those rich, smelly juices were blasted out when you cast out. Obviously as I have already said bait clips have been a real boon and they certainly allow long casts to be made with most baits, as does the 'Baitsafe' capsule but the way you bait up your hooks is still important for attracting the fish to the bait and finally catching them.

Lugworm You should have no problem with these unless they are the most watery of blow lug. Thread the worms onto the hook either head first or tail first whichever you prefer taking care not to puncture the worm along its body because this can start a split. Large black lug can be used singly or even cut into smaller pieces for flatfish etc. because their tough skins and the fact that they have been gutted keeps them firm and in one piece. Blow lug can be used either singly for small fish or in larger bunches depending on how big a bait you want.

One point to bear in mind however is that the bait should be kept as close to the hook point as possible because the further it is spread out the greater the chance of a fish hitting the snood and missing the hook altogether. With single small worms or small sections of black lug there is no real problem but once the bait exceeds about six inches in length the chances of a missed bite increases dramatically.

Basically you can overcome this in two ways, a) use another free sliding hook on the snood, which can be adjusted and positioned depending on bait size to give two hooks in one bait or b) to put a stop knot on the hook snood, bait up with several worms then compress them so that they form a shorter but fatter bait. With a) the worms remain fairly strung out and therefore more aerodynamic and by using a large hook on the end and a smaller hook on the snood you can catch large and small fish equally well. The bait does however look a bit like a barbed wire fence and you could of course hook a good fish on the small hook and lose it. With b) you really need to use large, long shanked hooks such as a 6/0 Aberdeen and try to compress most of the worms onto the shank. The bait then of course is quite fat and not nearly as aerodynamic as a single slim worm which is noticably up on distance into head winds. However the success rate of bites/fish is very high indeed.

Ragworm Of the three species that concern the beach angler the king and silver ragworm are the ones used most often and they are the toughest.

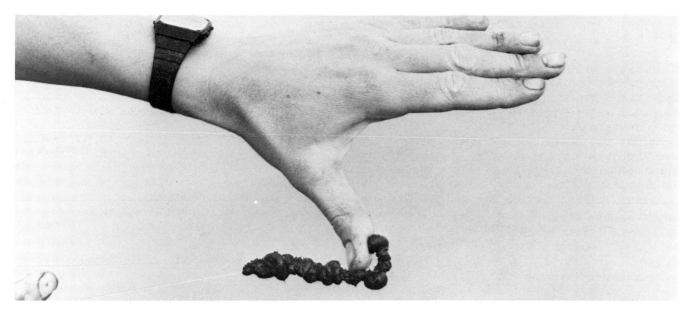

After threading the worms up the line slide the stop-knot to compress the worms into a 'ball'.

Both species seem to work better in areas where there is a least reasonable visibility which seems to indicate a bait that has a great deal of sight appeal.

If sight attraction is a factor then it may pay to

Hooked on the bait clip and positioned tight behind the sinker the bait is ready to be cast.

mount the worm onto the hook in such a way as to keep it alive and allow it to squirm in an attractive manner. The trouble is of course when long casting is called for. There is only one secure method and that is to thread the worm onto the hook and up the snood through the centre of its body. This effectively kills the worm anyway which tends to limit movement somewhat! Once the bait exceeds about six inches long I use another hook on the snood to hold the worm straight and increase the chance of a successful strike. It also stops the worm from falling into an unattractive blob on the hook because although I actually try to achieve this with lugworm (which is a scent bait), I try to avoid it with ragworm due to their sight attraction. Silver ragworm are better in this respect than king ragworm because they are a more muscular worm and retain their rigidity quite well.

For shorter casts the worms can be hooked in a lighter manner which does not kill them and which therefore retains movement. With very small sized worms and also with harbour ragworm the best way to hook them is to simply pierce them through the head end just once. By sliding up to twenty worms onto the hook shank and snood you end up with a writhing mass that proves irresistible to any species but particularly flounders. Some anglers prefer to slide the hook through the worm for a short distance rather than the straight through method but this does start a small tear in the worm and increases the chance of them being cast off. Mind you with this method of hooking casting ranges in excess of around 80 yds are almost impossible anyway so it is strictly a short range method. Larger worms can be mounted on Pennell tackle with one hook slipped in behind the head and the other approximately three quarters of the way down. Again this allows the worm to move but to only be cast relatively short distances.

Crab One of the reasons why some anglers shy away from using this bait is because they feel it is difficult to attach successfully to the hook. However like all baits it is quite easy although a little time consuming and once you have used it a few times it becomes second nature. The first considerations are as always the species of fish you are after and the distance to be cast because these make quite a difference to the preparation needed.

For long range casting the bait needs to be securely fixed to the hook and the best way to do this is to use elasticated thread. First of all kill the crab by piercing it in the head and then remove all the legs. These can be peeled and laid to one side to help secure the main body when it is in place on the hook. Next completely peel the crab removing all or as much of the body shell as possible and even cut out the old gills which are situated around the edge of the main body just above the leg sockets. Depending on the size of the crab and the fish to be caught you can leave it whole, cut it in half or even in quarters. Then take some elasticated thread, the finer the better, and wind it around the piece of crab from end to end. Being very soft the elasticated thread will squeeze the piece of crab into a stubby cigar-like shape and some of those lovely fish attracting juices will start to ooze out. Having done this you can simply thread the bait, from one end to the other onto the hook shank just like a piece of lugworm. Two or three legs can be threaded behind it to keep it in position and although it may not look much like a crab certainly smells like one and stays on the hook exceptionally well.

You can simply hold your hook against the piece of crab and bind the lot in one go but I find this a bit fiddly trying to hold both hook and bait together. By doing the bait first several pieces can be prepared and the hook baited very quickly indeed. For close range fishing you may be able to do without the complications of elasticated thread altogether, particularly in flounder matches where speed is a priority. In this case the hook should be passed through from the top shell to the bottom, back through the bottom to the top and so on depending on hook and bait size. By threading it on in this 'sewing' fashion the bait will stay in place, with the addition of a leg or two as well, for casts of up to 70–80 yds. Above this the bait breaks up.

For close range fishing for bass, particularly where the water is clear I like to use the crab whole. All I do here is to remove the top shell then pierce the hook straight through the centre of the body from the underside. The legs on one side are then gathered around the shank of the hook and whipped to it by a few turns of elasticated thread. A few turns of thread are also wound around the body to keep the soft new top shell in place. Otherwise the eels move in and pull the centre of the bait to pieces leaving you with a leggy skeleton. There seems little point in de-shelling the crab any further because the bass must often find them in this state and seem to take them readily. Also the softer the bait the more securing with elasticated thread it will need. Mounted this way 100 yd casts are easily possible.

Hermit crabs have to be removed from the shell first and then you can either use them whole for big fish or just the body section for smaller species. Either way the body is threaded the centre starting at the tail and emerging through at the head end. For long casting elasticated thread is again a must and can be wound along the body to hold it together and securely in place on the hook shank.

Shellfish Mounting shellfish depends largely on the species being used as bait. Razorfish with their long, thin tough bodies can be threaded onto the hook in the same manner as a worm and will withstand hard casting without further assistance. Just about all the other species used for bait – mussels, cockles, butterfish, limpets etc. have bodies consisting of some fairly firm pieces and the rest very loose and watery. To mount these successfully for long casting is very difficult but start out by removing them from the shell and laying them out on newspaper for a few minutes to dry them off a bit. This firms them slightly and then pierce the hook through the firmest pieces you can find and try to wrap the rest around the shank. After you have put on a few you will have a very mushy, jelly-like mass and this should be bound several times with elasticated thread to keep it in place. Surprisingly, although it looks fragile and some is bound to come off, you can cast the softest species such as mussel 120–130 yds quite successfully. Above this range I would start to look at alternative methods using the Baitsafe capsule.

The same problem exists with shrimps and prawns because although hooking through the tail segment is all right for float fishing and very short range they will soon fly off if any pressure is applied. You can mount them by passing the hook through the centre of the body, as a worm from head to tail or tail to head whichever you prefer and this is good enough for about 100 yard casts. Above that the Baitsafe would again be the answer.

Fish Baits The first thing to consider with fish baits is the size of bait you want to use. Conger and tope could require a complete side fillet of a mackerel or herring, and whiting only a thin strip. Whichever it is the bait should lie flat and even and not collapse into an unappetising blob on the bend of the hook.

To prepare a large bait simply run your knife along the flank of the fish completely removing one side to give a triangular shaped fillet. This is mounted by pushing the hook through from one side to the other at the tail end then threading it through for another three or four times depending on its size, sewing fashion until the hook finishes at the head end. To hold it in this position a short length of elasticated thread can be wrapped around the fillet at the tail end to hold it tight against the line. Alternatively you can use a second smaller hook on the snood and pass this through the tail end a couple of times to hold it out straight.

For smaller baits the fillet should be sliced to give the size required. The hook is then passed through the bait from one side to the other and slid up the snood to give you a bit of slack. The hook should then be taken round to the same side and pushed through again before threading it down the strip in a sewing motion. By giving the snood a pull the loop of line which you have put around the top of the bait will pull tight and grip the skin thereby ensuring that it retains its attractive shape. This is the method I use for fairly short strips and it works well but for long thin strips over 4–5 inches I would use the two hook arrangement to increase the chance of a successful strike.

With small fish such as sprats, whitebait or even sandeels the hook should be passed through the centre of the bait in a similar manner to worms. A baiting needle makes the job easier with sprats and whitebait with a few turns around the tail to hold it in position on the hook snood. Sandeels can be threaded on quite successfully without the help of a baiting needle because of their slim shape. Small eels can be used whole and larger ones cut in half to give nice sized pieces. Of course you won't want to do this if they are to be used live but again the method involved makes distance casting out of the question. For live eels the hook is pushed into the mouth then out through the lower jaw. Finally it is lightly nicked through the belly to hold the hook in place but not kill the eel.

Squid is the final fish bait to be mentioned and this is treated in the same manner as mackerel and herring. Used whole the hook should be passed through the centre of the body from the tail end and brought out at the head end. The tail should then be secured with elasticated thread or a second hook to ensure a natural appearance. The body can be opened out and cut into strips for small baits along with the tentacles and these are mounted in the same manner as fish strips.

As I stated at the beginning of this section the main priority is to keep the bait on the hook because without that you will catch nothing. As distance becomes less essential and water clarity increases, the way the bait looks may be given consideration because it may possibly make a difference. However life in the sea is hard and as long as the bait is in reasonable condition it ought to be effective. On this theme it pays to get as good

bait as you can and then keep it in good condition. It is heat that destroys most baits so always keep them out of the sun otherwise that lovely freshly caught mackerel will end up like a dried lump of leather.

Casting on the Beach Learning to cast on a field is certainly the best way but the difference between that and actually casting on the beach is quite a bit. On the field you've probably got a nice day with any wind coming from behind, light clothing, flat ground and a firm foothold. On the beach you have to cast in all sorts of weather with the wind very often coming straight at you or at best side-on, plenty of warm clothing on, steeply shelving ground and anything but a firm foothold. You can soon gather from this that your casting is not going to reach the standard you may have expected. Even trying a trace and imitation bait on the field is going to give a false result because with all the other factors against you it is impossible to apply yourself fully. In fact some very good tournament casters I know really struggle when fishing to achieve anything more than an average distance.

In the fishing situation the considerations have to be where to cast for effectiveness and safety. On flat sandy beaches where the tide moves in and out a fair distance casting can be fairly easy. If it is calm then you can stand right next to or just in the water where the sand should be fairly firm and there are not likely to be other anglers immediately on your casting side as they will have set their tackle up, back from the water line. On beaches which have a moderate slope on them the situation is usually fairly similar. Due to tidal movement the other anglers should be well back from the water's edge and just moving the rod through the casting arc a little higher should keep the sinker clear of the beach with only a small loss in distance. Often however the contours of the beach show small build-ups and depressions as you move away from the water line and by standing so that the rod tip passes over the depression you can move the rod as normal. A few yards back from the water line lessens the chance of the sinker hitting the beach and the better technique easily makes up those few yards.

Beaches that shelve very steeply can pose problems particularly for anglers who prefer rods in excess of 12 feet in length. Because the ground rises quickly it reduces the clearance between the rod tip and beach significantly making pendulum and back-cast techniques very difficult. If the beach rises evenly then the only answer is to find a reasonable foothold, shorten the drop slightly and move the rod through the arc in a higher plane. This obviously limits the compression built up in the rod but it is a case of making the most out of a bad job. Still, reasonable distances can still be achieved, certainly better than by giving it an 'overhead-thump'. Some of the steep shingle beaches go up with slight 'steps' every now and then and it can pay to move away from the water's edge and cast near one of these. Problems can arise due to other anglers setting up 'camp' on these 'steps' thereby putting them in a potentially dangerous area. The trouble is that on most of these beaches the tide only moves a short distance and therefore anglers tend to crowd the water's edge leaving no safety area for casting. Personally I set-up several yards back to leave plenty of room and always ask a neighbour to move back slightly while I cast because it is just not worth taking any risks.

Casting Angle Another point to consider when you cast from the beach is to vary the angle at which the sinker leaves the rod to allow for different wind conditions. In very calm weather the angle won't affect distance too much unless it is either ridiculously low or high, but in strong winds it can make a difference. Headwinds can make casting difficult particularly for multiplier users who have not set their reels up properly. The extra braking effect of the wind acts on the terminal tackle slowing it down very quickly and causing overruns on free running reels. Heavier sinkers help to some extent because of their slower but more even speed through the air but the best answer is to cast much lower than normal. This reduces the overall effect of the wind on terminal tackle and main line so that you can get as far as possible in the conditions.

Side winds are not quite as bad but they do tend to blow the main line out in a massive bow. This means that the reel has to supply a great deal more line than the straightforward distance would normally require. Therefore if your multiplier is over-braked it will not feed the line quickly enough and drag the sinker back. The same effect will occur with an underfilled fixed-spool because the level will drop very low causing excessive friction and retarding the sinker's progress. Thin main line is an advantage because by keeping the cross sectional area to a minimum the dragging effect of the wind is reduced. As with a head wind it pays to cast in a slightly lower trajectory than normal thereby keeping the amount of line hanging in the air to a minimum and reducing the force of the wind acting on the terminal tackle.

By far the nicest conditions are with a tail wind, not too strong but a steady breeze. The effect of this is to give additional lift to the baited trace so that maximum range is attained. By casting slightly higher than normal you can exploit this additional carrying power to its limit. When using soft baits, good conditions also help to preserve presentation by reducing the amount of casting power for a given distance.

Where to Cast Having picked the spot that you wish to fish you will almost certainly already have some idea where you want your bait to land. Whether this is at maximum range or into a gulley matters little but what is important is that it should stay there. I have fished alongside experienced anglers, who have obviously gone to great lengths to perfect most aspects of their fishing but who lose out because their tackle doesn't stay in the intended spot. It is not much good going to the trouble of selecting the best place on the best tide only to end up with your bait fishing well away from its desired position.

In some areas there is very little in the way of tidal flow and a sinker with sufficient weight to enable you to cast the required distance and combat the weather conditions is all you really need. Cast it straight to the spot and it should stay there. However in many other areas around the British coastline there are very strong tidal flows that run parallel with the beach as I have already stated and these can play havoc with inexperienced angler's tackle. The constant pressure of the water acting on the terminal tackle and main line will soon drag your bait well away from the fish. An answer could be to increase sinker weight but to keep this to the lowest level that you can it is better to cast the terminal tackle into a position up-tide of where you are on the beach. This allows the spikes to get a much better grip because the line forms a large 'bow' and helps to pull the sinker harder into the bottom. Therefore instead of having to use 6, 7 or even 8 oz you can still get away with 5–5½ oz which is better from a sporting viewpoint. Of course there will always be certain venues that experience very strong tides and these will always require the use of heavy sinkers but casting correctly makes a great deal of difference.

It is not at all uncommon to see anglers taking no account of the tide and proceeding to cast straight out from their fishing position. The result is that their trace is swept steadily down tide until it actually hits a snag, tangles with a neighbour's line or just swings in to about half the original distance cast. The way to stop this is to angle the cast into the tide or even walk ten to twenty yards up-tide and cast from there. Exactly how far you have to go will depend on the tide strength and sometimes the wind direction. Once the tackle has hit the sea bed let the line remain slack and do not tighten it up for a minute or so. This allows the tide to bow the line and the sinker to get a good grip. By the time everything has settled the line should be entering the water virtually straight in front of you and be nice and tight due to the tide acting on it.

Problems can arise on very crowded venues because of the limited space between anglers. However if the anglers fishing immediately up-tide of you are casting shorter than you it is possible to walk past a couple, cast out, then return to your

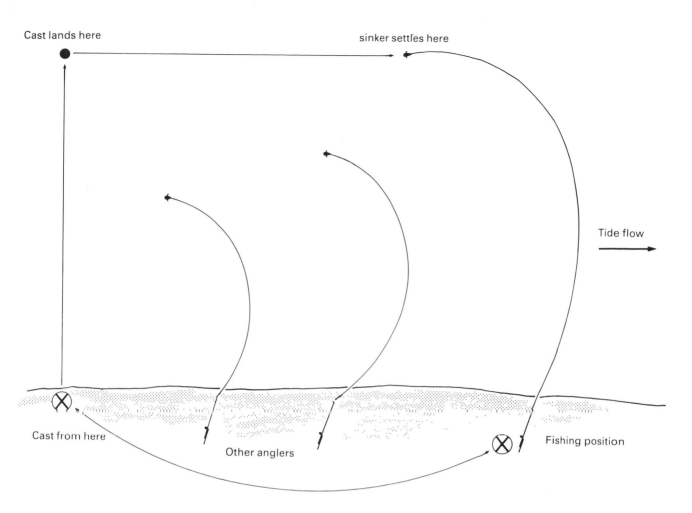

Cast lands here

sinker settles here

Tide flow

Cast from here

Other anglers

Fishing position

position passing your rod over their's as you go. Your sinker and line will then be pulled by the tide past their lines thereby enabling you to hold out straight and also reel in without catching anybody else. Often I have had to go past three or four other anglers to cast and they seem somewhat bewildered when I reel in without catching their lines. Mind you if a few fish do come your way they may accuse you of catching their fish before they get a chance to move further inshore, so watch out!

Basic Ledgering Techniques Casting up tide and 'nailing' the bait hard to the sea bed is the standard and regularly successful way of fishing beaches that have strong lateral flows particularly when there are a few other anglers about. Most 'round' fish such as cod, bass and whiting actively hunt out food, moving around in the flowing water searching out natural larders such as small holes, gullies and worm beds etc. With your bait held on the bottom sending out a steady scent trial down tide there is a fair chance that a fish will swim into it, pick it up then follow it to the source. That is of

course as long as you are fishing in the general area where the fish are.

Within these general areas however there are obviously going to be hotspots and these areas are going to produce the most fish. If the hotspot is a fairly wide gulley then you may be able to cast directly into it but there are often much smaller areas which are virtually impossible to cast to accurately at long range. The only practical way is to cast up tide of the spot and let your tackle slowly drift across into it. This can be achieved by varying the weight of the sinker or shortening them slightly so the terminal tackle just moves – but only just. It isn't any good letting your trace swing round quickly because it will just as easily swing straight past and only fish in the hotspot for a very short time. By moving it very slowly there is a good chance that as soon as it reaches a small depression it will lodge there for a while. I would aim for a movement that went from the casting point to a position where I had to reel in in about fifteen minutes.

As the strength of the tide reduces so you can

AREA COVERED BY ROLLING SINKER

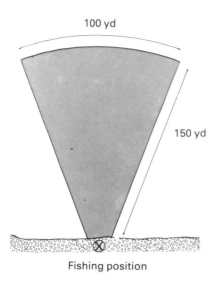

100 yd

150 yd

Fishing position

Shaded area shows tremendous amount of ground that can be covered with a rolling sinker.

use shorter spiked sinkers or even a pyramid and right next to slack water a plain bomb can give the movement required plus a few extra yards on your cast. By varying the distance cast letting the sinker slowly move round an enormous amount of ground can be covered. With two rods I normally put one well out then search about with the other. If a hotspot is found then both rods can be moved into the same area to maximise the catch potential. The greater the amount of ground searched the greater the chance of you finding feeding fish and then catching them.

With some species, notably flatfish, a moving bait can be a positive advantage. To begin with they usually bury themselves into the sand while the tide runs strongly picking up bits of food as they come into reach. Flatfish also tend to be inquisitive and small puffs of sand can entice them out of their hide to investigate. Therefore a moving lead is more likely to search out these hides and the bottom disturbance should also prove attractive. Near slack water gently reeling a couple of feet at a time with a pyramid lead will produce the same effect. With a moving lead however the point to remember is that you really do need a bit of room to search properly so a Saturday night when the cod are 'in' at Dungeness is not the place to try it out!

Bite Detection From the success of commercial long lines it is obvious that left to their own devices sea fish can make an efficient job of hooking themselves. This may be partly due to the fact there are more fish offshore and with all the competitors

for food there is only one, quick chance to swallow an item of food. Even from the shore there are days when large shoals of fish move in, feeding vigorously and no matter how bad your terminal tackle, coarse and blunt your hook and poor your bait, the fish will still oblige by 'hanging' themselves on the end. However with fish stocks gradually dwindling these dream days happen less and less often and more usually only a limited number of fish are going to move within casting range on a particular tide. At these times the more experienced and skilful angler will be more successful than the novice because neat tangle-free traces, sharp hooks, good bait, above average casting ability and being able to detect bites will all give him the advantage.

The most sensitive method for detecting bites has got to be holding the line and feeling for tugs and alterations in tension. However for sea fish this is really too sensitive and unnecessary. By holding the line you would probably tend to strike at the first indication of a bite which with many species would pull the hook out of the fish's mouth before it had a chance to take the bait properly. Also once the fish has made its mind up to take the bait it usually does so quite voraciously and the alteration in line tension shows clearly on the rod tip.

A rod rest is more than adequate for most situations so that the main part of the rod is held steady and the tip can move freely. If you are one of the many anglers who like to use two rods, especially a matched pair, it is a good idea to angle the rests so that the tips are very close together. By arranging them in this fashion you can compare one with the other, rather like a freshwater angler's target board, so that any changes in position show clearly. If the rod tip is by itself and set against a plain background such as when night fishing it is surprising how far it can alter without being noticed. Real 'wallops' will always be seen but more subtle bites such as a slight slackening of the line do not show up very well at all.

The first thing to do is to set the rod tips high enough to keep the line clear of the waves thereby avoiding any 'false' bites. Then tighten up to the sinker so that the line tension puts a good bend in the rod tip. This is the nice thing with fast taper rod blanks, the slim flexible tips take on a good set and show any movements up very clearly. Basically a bite will show up because there is a change in the line tension and the way the bite appears will depend on the state of the tide, the distance cast and the species of fish involved. Small fish such as whiting, pouting and flatfish tend to attack a bait in short bursts giving rises to a series of sharp tugs or 'rattles' on the rod tip. These show up quite clearly at close and medium range but once you get above about 120 yds the bow and inherent stretch in the line tends to absorb them so the rod tip movement is far less pronounced. Larger fish have more

Placing the rod tips close together clearly shows even small pulls or other changes in line tension.

confidence and move straight in once they have decided that the bait is acceptable. This gives a single solid pull on the rod tip which is clearly visible at almost any range.

With the tide running through bites are usually quite positive from all species perhaps because they think the bait may get swept away if they take too long. By setting your tackle up-tide as described in the previous chapter the added pressure of a fish pulling against the sinker is enough to pull it completely out of the bottom or at least move it a short distance. This will show clearly by a straightening of the rod tip giving the classic 'slack-line' bite that cod anglers know so well. Surprisingly even quite small fish can move the sinker. Although the sinker will normally hold the small additional pressure of a fish is just too much and it lets go. As the tide slackens the fish can become slightly less agressive as though they have more time and as slack water approaches a more keen attitude must be adopted to pick out smaller rod movements.

Striking This is often an emotive subject among sea anglers, some of whom say that striking is a waste of time while others swear that it is essential. Going back to the success of longlines it is obvious that the fish can hook themselves without striking but again shore fishing does not always conform to the same rules. The way to decide is to analyse the particular species, venue, conditions and casting distance and work out for yourself how important it is.

At fairly close range up to 100 yds, there could be a case for striking particularly with shy biting fish that spit out a bait as soon as some resistance is felt. Rock bass are a good example of this. With such a limited amount of line out and as long as the tidal flow isn't putting a ridiculous bow in the line a strike is going to move the sinker virtually straight away and possibly hook the fish. Once you get above this range particularly at 130 yds plus the time delay in seeing the bite, picking up the rod, taking up the slack and actually moving the sinker is going to mean that the fish is either already hooked or has gone. Even grabbing the rod, and rushing back up the beach like a madman has little effect; the bow and stretch in the line will absorb nearly all these efforts. It is obvious therefore that at long range striking is effectively a waste of time.

This is why flowing traces are useless in strong tides because their so called bite indication advantage just doesn't hold up. The idea of the fixed paternoster, wired sinkers and casting into the tide is to set up as effective a self hooking rig as possible. By using needle sharp hooks the point should lodge in the fish's mouth as soon as it tries to move away. The sinker will then provide enough anchorage to pull the fish up and sink the hook home. Even if it is not fully home at first it soon will be as the fish struggles to get free. With the tide running, few fish are generally missed but as the tide slows and the fish become less aggressive the percentage of missed bites increases. You can try striking if you want to but unfortunately these missed chances have to be accepted most of the time. This is when ultra sharp hook points pay off

because they need the minimum of pressure to slip home.

Playing and Landing a Fish   Now that the fish has been successfully hooked you want to ensure that it ends up on the beach. Any species of small fish should not pose any problems because they lack the physical size and strength to resist even the sinker weight let alone the force that is dragging them towards the shore. As long as the fish is reasonably well hooked you should have no difficulties. You will always drop a few but that is inevitable with any fishing. I have seen match anglers purposely reel in quickly to bring fish like pout, whiting and flatties up to the surface and then 'skitter' them across the surface. This is not my style but it looks good when speed is everything

Landing fish is easy for an experienced angler. Notice how he uses the incoming wave to push the fish up the beach while at the same time moving in close in case it comes off at the last moment.

and seconds cannot be wasted on a slow retrieve.

It is with larger fish that some care is necessary and judging by the mess you see some anglers making of landing something that actually pulls back, a bit of advice wouldn't go astray. The actual size and species of fish involved will determine how it fights but there really isn't any species swimming around British waters that should prove a problem, excluding sharks of course. Tope are probably the largest and fastest fish that the beach angler is likely to tackle but if you set out to catch them and use a reel with sufficient line capacity to cope with the long runs that they are well known for they can be handled as easily as most other species.

More often than not the 'fight' consists of a slow moving solid pull interspaced with a few short runs and some amount of head shaking. The fish's natural instincts tell it that all is not well and therefore it gets frightened and tries to get away. The angler, on the other hand, although excited, should stay as calm as possible. It is always a pleasant feeling when you pull the rod back and feel that heavy resistance on the other end and as long as you keep the line tight and the rod tip up there should be few problems.

Begin by tightening the line and raising the rod tip to apply a steady, firm pressure which puts a reasonable bend in the blank. This usually gets the fish moving towards the shore and short runs or sudden lunges can be absorbed by the line stretch and the flexibility of the rod tip. As long as the ground is fairly snag free this pressure should be maintained as you recover line and as the fish nears the shoreline any swell in the water can be use to good effect to help carry the fish further in. As the swell lifts the fish raise the rod to apply more pressure then slowly lower the tip slightly and retrieve line at the same time; this way the fish virtually swims in itself. Never haul and winch a fish in a direct tug of war; you might get away with this with a 6 lb fish but the hook could pull out or straighten with a double figure fish. The bigger the fish the more patience and more care you should apply. If the ground is snaggy you will have to keep the fish off the bottom and this will require a fair bit of pressure but in this case the line strength and hook size and strength should have already been chosen to take this into account.

Eventually the fish will arrive into a position just behind the breakers and in anything but calm seas this can be a critical time. More fish are lost in the final stage than at any other time and this is usually due to over-exuberance on the part of the angler, who is often trying to get the fish ashore too quickly. As the water shallows and the noise of the surf increases the fish will probably start to panic and pull harder. The undertow from the breaking waves will also be trying to pull the fish back out to sea and therefore considerable strain will be placed on the rod, reel, line and hook hold. However by keeping the line tight and applying pressure as the waves come in you will find that the fish will almost be washed ashore for you. By standing back from the water's edge and loosening the clutch slightly you should be able to cushion sudden pulls that occur as the undertow pulls the fish back. Obviously you can't just let it go back but don't just stand there and hold on for grim death because that's when you will lose it. Keep the rod tip up all the time also to cushion smaller lunges.

With the fish actually in the surf you can act positively and apply pressure. As the wave lifts it will sweep the fish towards the shore and the combination of pressure from you and the wave should beach the fish. Sometimes the fish doesn't quite make it far enough and the backwash tries to pull it back again. So as before cushion the pressure by walking towards the sea slightly or letting some line go, then repeat the process as the wash from the next wave rushes in. Once the fish is far enough up the beach it will be left high and dry for you to pick up. The steeper the beach gradient the harder it is to land fish in rough weather. Surf beaches gradually shallow out and you can easily

After landing a fish your line may look like this. If so, flick the sinker out and rewind it nice and level.

91

lead the fish ashore with the minimum of fuss but on steep-to venues quite a bit of pressure will have to be applied during the final stage and then is the time to hope for the best.

The rougher the sea the greater the risk of losing the fish. A large cod in a stormy winter sea not only uses its own strength but also the power of the undertow acting on its body to help it escape. However by being patient and keeping calm at all times you should be able to use the elements to help you as well and successfully land the fish. If you use a multiplier reel and hook a large fish you will be concentrating on landing it so much that your line laying will probably be rather more uneven than usual. So before re-casting just flick the sinker out, thumbing the line gently to clear it then reel it back so that it lies level. If you don't the next cast could go 200 yds – unattached!

Auxiliary Equipment

Apart from the rod and reel which are obviously the most important items for any angler there are many others which, although not critical to success contribute a great deal to comfortable and efficient angling. On warm summer days the very minimum of equipment and clothing would do but try the same on a cold, wet, windy winter's night and see how long you last. There are many pieces of equipment which the shore angler needs to acquire and it is just as well to spend a bit of time getting yourself well and truly organised; this always pays in the long run.

Tackle Boxes First on the list has got to be a decent sized tackle box or bag because this is going to be needed to transport all the small items of tackle to the beach. The choice between a bag or a box can largely depend on the type of terrain you usually fish. Rock areas or those venues that require very long walks to reach them are instances where a bag can be better particularly the large alloy framed models used by hikers. The frames are usually shaped to lie against the back and the bag itself, usually made from heavy duty nylon is secured to the other side. The bags are very spacious and are usually equipped with a number of additional pockets which are ideal for those smaller items. Because they are basically aimed at walkers they are very light and, probably more importantly, are very comfortable to carry – something that can't be said for most boxes. Camping shops are really the place to look because their choice is usually much greater than the tackle shop although they sometimes have a few, especially those which incorporate a folding chair.

Tackle shops will however, have a good selection of boxes and the choice is quite varied, from older wicker baskets to more modern wood, fibreglass and the very popular metal frame/nylon covered type. The old wicker baskets, once a very popular choice have lost favour amongst sea anglers because of their inability to keep out the number one enemies sand and salt water, which do so much damage to metal and moving parts.

Wooden boxes are better in this respect and being covered by nylon they last well. They do tend to be slightly on the heavy side and uncomfortable to carry long distances. The sharp edges where the side and bottom sections meet rub on the lower part of the back as you carry the box and the greater the weight the worse it becomes. Unfortunately the need to carry a number of sinkers means that the box is always heavy no matter how you try

and trim your equipment to the minimum. Fibreglass isn't as bad in this respect because the back panel is often shaped to lie against you better and the corners are also well rounded. They are also light and the only thing that stops them from being ideal is the fact that they only have a single strap. Twin straps spread the load far better and the metal framed, nylon covered models that have this feature are ideal even though they are rather expensive.

The nice thing about a box rather than a bag is that it maintains its shape so that everything can be laid out neatly and access is easy. Bags are not so rigid and at times can become a bit disorganised inside. Also most double up as a seat so there is no need to carry an extra chair for the periods when the fish are slow to feed.

Containers For the multitude of small items such as hooks, swivels, line clips, traces etc., you really need some sealable plastic bags and plastic containers – not metal ones. The old tobacco tins are all right when new but soon become rusty both inside and out when the sea air gets to them. The same goes for your hooks and swivels so keep them in sealable plastic bags while they are not required for use.

The plastic bags can then be kept in plastic containers such as Tuppaware, which again are well sealed against sand and water. With all the loose items in containers it is a simple matter to pack them neatly into the box ready for use as required. I even use the bottom part of a plastic maggot box to hold my sinkers so I know exactly how many of each type I've got rather than having to hunt about in the bottom of my box to find one.

Umbrellas and Shelters In some parts of the country it is very unfashionable to use an umbrella or such like shelter for beach fishing. Why I really don't know because they are invaluable in bad weather and quite honestly I wouldn't think of going fishing without taking mine. Certainly there are some areas where the tide moves vast distances in a very short period of time and in that case it would be very difficult to keep moving about. However in the depths of winter with a cold easterly blowing you could be sitting it out for one bite and to remain comfortable and enthusiastic some kind of shelter is a must.

Umbrellas are certainly the most popular being reasonably priced and easily transported. They take only a few moments to erect or dismantle and offer more than enough protection to keep both the angler and his tackle warm and dry. The only point to consider is the wind so ensure that all the time the canopy points into it. Once the umbrella has been sited kick up some sand or shingle around the bottom of the canopy to help stabilise it, and make sure that the guy ropes are well staked down.

Additional shelter can be obtained by wrapping a wind break around the umbrella, although it is more to carry, or by sewing 'wings' onto the sides. These 'wings' really do cut out a lot of draughts and are ideal for the all night angler who likes to make camp for a long session. In fact I think one manufacturer actually produces an umbrella complete with 'wings' as standard and although dismantling is made slightly more difficult, they are very good.

Rod Rests These are another vital piece of equipment for most beach angling situations. Certainly some venues and/or species are tackled better by holding the rod while the bait is fishing; surf beaches or rock bassing are examples, where direct contact between angler and fish can be essential for sensing shy bites and then reacting to them quickly. However for the general run of fish likely to be caught by the shore angler, particularly those species that are not renowned for lightning bites, the success rate is likely to be just as good or even better if they are given enough time to swallow the bait completely.

Good rod rests are not an item that many tackle shops seem to stock; they seem to think that any lump of angle iron will do. They do the job I suppose but soon get covered in rust and add weight that on a long walk you could well do without. Basically there are three different designs of rod rest; the monopod, the tripod and the lean-to. For all-round beach fishing the monopod is probably the best choice and on flat surf beaches where the water rushes a long way up the sand they are really the only practical choice. In these circumstances the rod is held securely and high enough to keep the line clear of breaking waves, which if laden with weed can make fishing all but impossible. The best monopods are made from alloy for corrosion resistance and light weight and consist of a three to four feet length of $1\frac{1}{4}$ inch angle with a semi-circular section of tubing placed at the top and a full cup positioned approximately halfway between top and bottom (see diagram).

Another good beach rest is the lean-to but these perform best where there is little chance of the water reaching them, i.e. medium to steep-to venues. Although they can be arranged to hold the rod tip fairly high it isn't as high as a monopod and certainly not as secure if the water keeps washing around the rod handle, continually knocking it about. Again most of those sold by tackle shops tend to be made from steel but you can easily make your own from dural tube (see diagram), which is far better. The nice thing with this design is that when using two rods the tips can be positioned very close and thereby show bites up much better. The same can be done with monopods but it takes a bit of time to get the angle of each one just right.

MONOPOD ROD REST

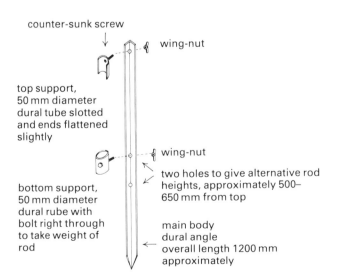

counter-sunk screw

wing-nut

top support, 50 mm diameter dural tube slotted and ends flattened slightly

wing-nut

two holes to give alternative rod heights, approximately 500–650 mm from top

bottom support, 50 mm diameter dural rube with bolt right through to take weight of rod

main body dural angle overall length 1200 mm approximately

Lean-to rod rests are popular in areas where tidal movement is relatively small.

94

Tripods are a free standing rest and as the name suggests that have three legs joined at the top. They are a vital piece of equipment if you fish areas where it is impossible to push a monopod or lean-to rest into the ground, such as harbours, piers and rock ledges. I do not like them for general beach work because it is virtually impossible to keep the rod tip high and retain stability. Excessive pressure from weed, strong tides or even a good bite usually topples the lot and surf beaches are obviously out. Therefore unless the sea is flat calm I wouldn't want to use one although on harbours etc, the additional height of the structure does the job of keeping the line clear anyway.

Pressure Lamps The type of pressure lamp seen on beaches now has changed considerably in the last few years especially with the cheap imports from China. At one time the only type to buy was the Tilley Stormlight, a very simple and robust design that gave years of reliable service with only the minimum of maintenance. The light output was I think, around 250 candlepower, although I must admit it seemed to vary quite a bit from lamp to lamp, and although not fantastic it was enough to fish reasonably easily. Tilleys are a reasonable buy if you can get hold of one second hand but their new price makes them rather expensive for what you get.

Most keen anglers and certainly those who do any amount of night fishing go for the more modern Anchor, Optimus and Coleman lanterns which give twice as much light output as the Tilley. The Coleman is the least popular and this is probably due to a lack of advertising and general availability in most tackle shops. Also it lacks the quick start facility of the other two and this feature is a definite advantage when you want to get fishing in a hurry.

The Optimus has been around a few years now and is unmistakable in appearance. Made in Sweden its tall chromed brass body stands out a mile and so does its light output. Coupled with the quick start I must admit that this lamp made night fishing much more enjoyable for me, you could actually see what you were doing! The only minus point with the Optimus is its price. They have always been quite expensive but in the last couple of years the price has really rocketed leaving the market open for the latest intruder, the Anchor. Anchor lamps are imported from China at an incredibly low price, well below that of a Tilley in fact and they are virtually a copy of the Optimus. In fact many parts are interchangeable between the two although there is no doubt that the Anchor lacks the overall quality of the Optimus.

Operation of both these lanterns is very easy but there are of course disadvantages. Firstly, to keep them running sweetly they do require regular maintenance and will not tolerate neglect. Secondly, the mantle is held at one end only, rather like a

A good pressure lamp is a must for night fishing. Lamps like this Anchor are very powerful when compared to the older Tilleys.

light bulb in fact and therefore sharp knocks will fracture it very easily and this can get rather expensive. Finally a high light output requires fuel and therefore the Optimus and Anchor lamps will only give about seven to eight hours burning against twelve for a Tilley. This is all right for most anglers but not enough for the all night enthusiast. Of course the running cost will also be higher but that is a small price to pay for a better light.

Some rod rests have hooks or similar attachments to hold a pressure lantern. However I prefer to use a separate lamp holder so that I can position it to get the maximum illumination for both bite detection and casting. For my lamp I use a six foot length of one inch dural angle which has two small slots in the top to hold the handle securely and stop the lamp swinging about. Although it is a fairly sizable piece of equipment it is still light and certainly doesn't match the weight of some of the stands that I've seen used.

When it is really cold and windy I usually keep the lamp behind the umbrella on the ground. Although the light spread is reduced the wind eddies round and under the canopy trapping the warm air. Even on very cold nights it can get quite

LAMP STAND

slots cut in top to hold
lamp handle

main body 1″ dural angle length
2 m approximately. Angle
supports lamp base to avoid
turning and swinging about

warm which certainly makes fishing much more
pleasant.

Gaffs and Nets These items are of very limited
use for the shore angler and really a gaff isn't
necessary at all for landing fish from the beach.
We've all seen pictures of the proud angler lifting
the fish out of the surf using a gaff but in practice it
is extremely difficult to do this. Fish rarely stay still
long enough to get the gaff into them particularly
when the weather is rough. At a couple of venues I
fish there is a five to six feet high wooden break-
water running parallel with the tideline that protects the ever crumbling cliffs from the sea. Sometimes you have to fish behind this sea defence and
landing fish is very difficult. In this situation a gaff
can be handy for dragging big fish up and over the
woodwork but for general open beaches a careful
approach is all that is needed as described in the
Fishing Techniques section.

From piers and harbour walls the only safe way
to land very large fish is to use a drop net. Smaller
fish can be handlined up but even then you always
risk them dropping off. The nets stocked by most
tackle shops are usually too small and really the
only answer is to make one yourself. A large
circular or triangular frame with a span in the 3–4 ft
range is best, coupled with good strong heavy duty
netting. The idea is to lower the net just below the
surface draw the fish across it and then lift it cleanly
out. Sounds easy but I can assure you it isn't and
only practice makes perfect.

Protective Clothing Although you may be able to
go fishing during the summer wearing only the
minimum of clothing the weather in this country
usually calls for some sort of protective clothing.
Wet, windy winter nights are probably the worst
time for shore angling and to retain full use of your
body it is going to need to be kept both warm and
dry. A cold miserable angler is soon going to get
fed up if the fish are slow to feed and his concentra-
tion will never match the chap who is wearing
clothing that retains body heat and keeps water
out.

An absolute necessity for any angler is a good
set of thermal underwear. Most large stores stock
some sort or another and I'm sure you've had
leaflets put through the door from companies like
Damart. It really is well worth the money being
light, comfortable to wear and extremely efficient
when it comes to keeping a warm layer of air next
to the skin. It is also designed to let moisture
through which is an important factor in keeping the
skin warm. Most venues require some sort of walk
to reach them and no matter how cold the outside
air your skin soon heats up and sweats. Once you
have reached your position the skin cools and if the
moisture hasn't been able to get away it also cools
making you feel chilly and generally uncomfortable.

On top of this a shirt and sweaters can be worn
and then over the lot a good wind/water proof suit
or jacket and overtrousers. In really wet weather a
one piece suit is best in keeping you dry although
they do restrict movement for casting to some
degree. When the weather is more showery and
not too cold one piece suits can become exceptionally warm and rather a nuisance to keep taking
off. Therefore some anglers prefer a jacket and
separate leggings so that they only need wear the
necessary garment. Whichever you prefer make
sure that it is 100% waterproof and stamped to say
so. Too many so called waterproof coats end up
leaking in really heavy rain and usually it is worth
spending the extra money on guaranteed clothing.
Most of the really good suits and coats are made
from nylon which has been specially treated or
backed with either rubber or p.v.c. I managed to get
hold of a very good suit from a rig worker friend
which is also treated on the inside to stop sweat
building up. It is the only waterproof that I have
ever used that keeps me 100% dry and I believe it
retails under the name of Drytex made by Faithful
of Worcester and costs about £35.

As far as footwear is concerned every shore
angler needs a pair of waders. A very large proportion of time is spent either in or very close to the
sea and usually in conditions which would soon fill
a pair of short boots. Waders are fairly expensive
and really need to be looked after to avoid de-
terioration and leakage. Never leave them for long
periods with the top half folded down otherwise

the rubber will crease and eventually split. The best way is to find a way of hanging them upside down and straight. Be sure to buy a pair which are one or even two sizes too big so that you have plenty of room to put on a couple of pairs of thick socks. With socks on the boots should be a firm fit but not tight. Tight boots result in cold feet.

Shorter rubber boots or more particularly those that are insulated inside such as Derriboots or 'moon' boots are useful for rocks, piers or days when the sea is very calm. Waders can be unpleasant on a long walk so shorter boots are useful to have. However if it is likely to be rough a choice has to be made between comfort for walking or comfort for fishing.

Incidentals Pliers and Forceps – apart from flatfish most species have some form of teeth, not massive things of course but rows of small needle heads that soon tear your skin if you push your finger into its mouth when unhooking. A pair of forceps or long nosed pliers will allow you to reach into the throat of a deeply hooked fish and dislodge the hook easily. Pliers are also handy of course for any minor repairs that may be needed to equipment during the session.

Knives Another very important item which is called upon to do a variety of essential jobs. Cutting and filleting fish, cutting out tangled line are all jobs that require a good, strong and not too flimsy a knife. Again good quality is worth paying for so that the knife retains its edge and does not become blunt easily.

For trimming line when making traces or tying on a new leader nail cutters are very good and certainly easier than a knife. Some tackle shops stock them but if not try Woolworths or any other general store.

Sharpening Stones – handy for sharpening your knife and most importantly your hooks. Check the hooks after every cast to keep them sharp because even a light brush against a stone will soon take the edge off the point.

Scales Most anglers like to know the weight of a good fish and judging from some of the 'guessing' I've seen many would be better to make sure. You can choose either straight spring balances or dial

Nail clippers are the ideal tool for trimming line ends.

guage types. Spring balances are usually cheaper and quite adequate for a general indication of the weight of a fish but if you want to weigh in club matches then the dial type is likely to be more accurate. The higher the rating of the scales the coarser the graduations are likely to be and a 20 lb set ought to be enough for individual fish. Above that weight the fish warrants official weighing at a tackle shop especially in the case of records or fish to be entered in competitions. In these cases witnesses must be present.

Accessories often do not get the attention they deserve. The idea is to make your trips more comfortable, organised and therefore efficient. A warm angler fishes longer and enjoys himself far more whether the fish are feeding keenly or not and generally catches far more than the chap who arrives with the basics or unreliable equipment. The unprepared angler gets fed up quickly whereas the prepared angler doesn't and consequently does better in catching fish which, after all, is the object of the game.

Maintenance

Today nothing is obtained cheaply and usually you only get what you pay for in terms of performance and quality. Fishing tackle obeys this rule in the same way as virtually every other product and therefore to the average person a rod and reel represents a considerable outlay in hard-earned cash. Therefore it is only common sense to take very special care of rods, reels and all the many other items you use, otherwise the salt air and sand will corrode and sieze-up anything neglected.

Looking after equipment takes only a very short time and time spent on maintenance is certainly well spent, paying dividends in terms of trouble free use and overall reliability. Nothing is worse than having your tackle let you down on the beach particularly when it tends to be an extremely cold, wet and windy night or when you've got that fish of a life-time on. Regular checks and cleaning reduce the chance of a let down by siezed clutches, broken rings, pressure lamps failing to light or the many other small but nevertheless annoying faults that can disrupt a fishing session.

Rods Because a rod does not consist of numbers of moving parts it probably gets more neglect and abuse than any other single item. Although the blank is made from a corrosion resistant material such as glass, carbon or a mixture of both it still requires a quick check after each session. Even When you first buy the rod it pays to inspect it closely for any flaws which could have occurred in manufacture or transit. The last thing you want is for the rod to fall in half on the first cast even if you are going to get it replaced under guarantee. Have a look along the complete length of the blank looking for cracks in the material or marks where excessive pressure could have been exerted. Any of these could prove a weak spot under the pressures of hard casting.

The same check should be done after each trip to ensure that any sharp knocks or careless handling when loading the car haven't set-up hairline cracks. Carbon in particular is liable to this sort of damage because of the brittle nature of this material so extra care with handling is needed here, plus of course good insurance! Whether your rod is carbon or glass it is worth keeping it in a rod bag for storage and transit because even though the material is only relatively thin it will still take the sting out of a sharp blow and may save the rod from serious damage.

The line guides protrude well out from the blank and are therefore another part of the rod liable to damage. Again they should be checked on a new rod before you take it out of the shop or even if you buy them loose to build a rod yourself. Currently the selection is quite good and a great deal of progress has been made in the past few years to produce good, hard wearing guides. Not that long ago the choice was limited to porcelain lined or straight chromed wire guides and both designs were easily damaged.

Current designs are far better with the ceramic liner held in a plastic shock absorbing ring and wire frame being the most popular. This type of ring resists grooving exceptionally well and takes a lot of abuse, especially the three legged design. Even so a check for cracking is essential to avoid badly frayed or even cut line during use.

Such intensive rod care must seem like a lot of trouble but in reality it only takes a few minutes to give it a check over plus giving the reel fitting a quick squirt with W.D.40 or some similar water repellant/lubricating spray. A beachcasting rod takes a great deal of punishment during a season particularly when the angler continually needs to fish at long range, therefore you should be sure to treat it with the care and respect it deserves.

Reels Unlike the rod, a reel has a large number of moving parts and as such it is very vulnerable to the ingress of sand. With this in mind is pays to clean your reel thoroughly after each session to ensure a long working life and smooth operation.

Fixed-spool reels are fairly easy to keep clean when compared to a multiplier and this point makes a good selling point for beginners and the less serious angler. The first thing to do after a trip is to rinse the whole reel under a warm tap to wash off the worst of the sand and salt water. Once this is done remove the spool and wipe out any sand that has been trapped underneath – a soft paint brush is ideal for this. Finally spray the body with W.D.40, wipe off the excess and replace the spool. This takes about as long to do as it did to read about it yet adds years to the life of the reel.

At longer intervals, say 3–4 weeks, lightly oil the spindle where it emerges through the reel body and also the bail arm hinge points. Then once a year take the reel completely to pieces, wash out all the old grease with paraffin to get rid of any swarf particles and then re-grease and re-assemble. Again both quick easy jobs but ones that increase life expectancy and operating smoothness of the reel.

Multipliers, on the other hand, are a mass of

Regular WD40 treatments add years to a reel's life.

moving parts and really require regular maintenance if they are to be kept running smoothly. Their
life expectancy will also be dramatically reduced
if neglected, particularly the smaller bait casting
models which are currently popular with the majority of distance casters. These reels were originally
aimed at the freshwater market and although they
are currently accepted as the best type of multipliers to go for the manufacturers haven't bothered
to upgrade the specification to resist the ravages of
sand and salt water. Most of the larger purpose-
built sea fishing multipliers tend to be more robust
but less efficient for casting, but even so that
doesn't mean that you can neglect them, because
they will soon let you down if you do.

Many anglers avoid multipliers because of their
inherent casting problems, although modern braking systems have helped a great deal in this area,
yet I am sure that many more are put off at the
thought of ever having to take the reel apart. There
is no doubt that compared with a fixed-spool a
multiplier is certainly more complex but even so it
is still not beyond anyone's capability to strip it
down and reassemble it. Unless you buy the reel
second hand it should have a parts list and an
exploded diagram of the internals. By referring to
this you should be able to take the reel apart

without too much trouble which will allow a check
on the condition of the internals on an old reel and
a check for trapped metal particles on a new one.
The latter is quite common with today's mass
production techniques by the way. Another advantage of doing this strip and rebuild task is that it
allows you to become familiar with the way the reel
operates and should it play up on the beach you
will be in a far more confident position to make a
repair.

To keep your multiplier in peak condition it will
need a routine clean and check after every session.
Simply brush over the reel with a soft, long haired
paint brush to remove all sand particles and odd
pieces of weed. Then remove the drive side complete and the check side from the frame, then
finally the spool. Rinse the frame under a hot tap to
wash out the salt water being especially careful on
reels such as the Daiwa 6HM to clean the area
where the reel seat is fixed to the main frame. This
gap is very vulnerable to salt corrosion and it is not
unknown for the two pieces to break apart. Wipe
the spool over with a clean, dry cloth and place it to
one side so that the line doesn't get contaminated
with greasy substances, something that makes
gripping it virtually impossible. Next wipe the end
plates over before giving them a spray of W.D.40.

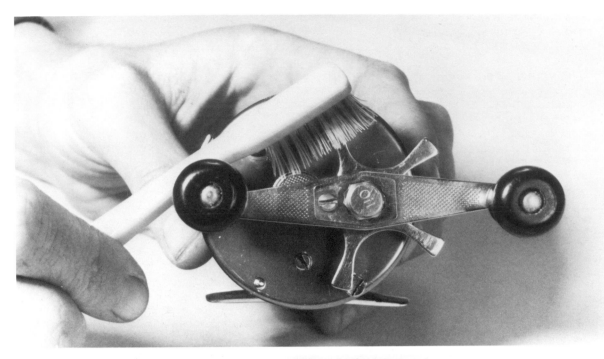

A toothbrush is ideal for removing sand and weed particles.

This is particularly important with reels that have alloy end plates because no matter how careful you are the anodised finish always get scratched allowing the salt to get at the metal. W.D.40 dilutes this salt, although it can never stop it completely and ensures that the plates last a great deal longer than they would if neglected. Leave the plates for an hour at least then wipe off the excess lubricant, assemble the reel, being sure to put a small drop of oil on the spool spindle where it passes through the drive gear. At longer intervals of about 10 sessions or so it pays to carry out a more comprehensive cleaning schedule. First remove all the main items – the drive side, check side and spool as you usually do but this time completely strip down the drive side and remove the bearings. Rinse all the components in paraffin or petrol to remove old oil, grease and sand and check carefully for wear. The most noticable wear will be on the small drive gear particularly the brass type used on the baitcasting multipliers. These are subject to a great deal of strain and the teeth have a pronounced hooked shape as they wear. They become thinner and thinner until eventually they strip completely and that is something you don't want to happen in use. Once the teeth look bad replace the gear. The larger drive gear may also be bad although I usually find that it survives about as long as two smaller gears.

All the parts should then be re-oiled and re-assembled with the bearings being thoroughly soaked in the grade of oil that you find most suitable for your technique and fishing situation (see section on *Reels*). Of course if you have a really nasty day with sand being blasted along the beach and therefore into your reel or it gets swamped in the sea then you will need to give the reel this complete strip. Nothing upsets a previously smooth reel more than being dunked. The water penetrates the bearings, washes out some of the oil and makes it run much faster often causing an overrun.

With both fixed-spool and multiplier reels it is a case of keeping the sand and salt water at bay. With only a little care this is very easily done and ensures that the reel performs its functions reliably for years.

Pressure Lanterns These are often a very neglected item and seem to have the nasty habit of letting you down at the most awkward time such as on a blustery winter's night. All the pressure lamps currently on the market work on the same principle of spraying vapourized paraffin onto a mantle where it is then burnt to give off light. The process itself is quite simple and straightforward yet it throws up a number of potential problems because of the fragile nature of the mantle and the sooty nature of the fuel used. Add to this the sand/salt environment of the beach and it is not difficult to see that a neglected lamp won't give the trouble free service that you really need. Whichever model you choose the maintenance routine follows the same basic pattern. After each session remove the handle, top cover and mantle holding assembly taking special care not to brush the mantle against anything or subject it to sharp knocks, otherwise you end up with a pile of dust instead of a mantle. Next take out the glass and remove the main frame

(Tilleys, by the way, have the frame fixed to the base and it cannot be removed) leaving you with the base and main stem. Take a hand brush and sweep over the base to remove all the sand particles and wipe over with a clean cloth. Alternatively you can quickly rinse over the base with fresh water to do the same job and also dilute any salt water that has become caught up in a seam. Having done that I also remove the pump plunger and put a small amount of oil or grease onto the leather washer. These washers tend to dry up after a while and if they are not lubricated you will find it impossible to pressurise the bowl. This is not a job that needs doing every time but certainly every 3–4 weeks if you use the lamp regularly.

At this point the bowl can be refilled with fuel and the other components wiped over with a clean cloth; extra care being taken with the mantle of course. Clean all the dirt and baked-on salt spray from the glass otherwise it will build up and greatly reduce the light output of the lamp. It is useless buying a lamp that gives out 500 candlepower yet only 250 candlepower emerges through a dirty glass. Once cleaned all the components can be reassembled with a final check of the mantle for any damage. It pays to be quite thorough with this examination because even a small hole means that the mantle needs replacing. The lamp may function quite well but you will find that the hole creates a hot spot on the glass opposite it and this can cause the glass to crack as it cools. The point is that a new mantle is a lot cheaper than a new glass!

No matter how careful you are you will need to replace the mantle on your lamp sooner or later. This is a simple, straightforward job but one which should be done properly if you want to avoid early damage, particularly with the bulb type mantles used on the Optimus, Anchor and Coleman lamps. Tilleys have a far more robust mantle because it is supported both at the top and the bottom and usually it requires a direct blow or very severe jolt to break it. If you do, however, the first job is to remove all fragments of the mantle left on the holder and give it a good blow out to remove any dust. The new mantle has a large and a small opening and the large one should be fitted uppermost onto the groove in the burner body. The smaller opening should be stretched over the short spigot that projects from the burner so that it is supported at the top and bottom. Finally arrange the fabric of the mantle evenly so that it takes on a nice shape as it is 'burnt off' and replace the burner assembly and the hood.

The pre-heating clip can then be placed on the lamp and the lighting procedure started. The flame from the clip will soon 'burn off' the mantle and once pre-heating of the stem is complete pump the bowl up to a reasonable pressure and turn the lamp on quickly. The sudden rush of vapourized paraffin should push the mantle outwards so that it takes up the nice even shape necessary for maximum efficiency.

Mantle replacement on the larger and more powerful Optimus, Anchor and Coleman lamps is very similar but more care is required to avoid early breakage. The mantle on these lamps is supported at the top end only and therefore it is very liable to damage. To avoid this damage especially with only minor knocks and bumps it is very important to get a nice even shape to the mantle and to do this the fabric should be arranged evenly before 'burning off' commences. If it is not the mantle takes on a 'lop-sided' shape when lighting pressure is applied and invariably breaks under the slightest provocation. It is much easier to even the fabric out if you assemble the lamp without the glass because as you assemble the lamp the mantle fabric has to be pushed through the ring at the top of the main stem. With the glass in-situ it is then impossible to spread out the fabric. I then burn the mantle off by holding a match under the fabric and only when this is complete do I follow the normal starting procedure. Then by turning the lamp on and off quickly a couple of times the mantle usually forms a nice even shape. Even so these perfectly formed mantles are still very fragile so handle with care.

Because of the sooty nature of paraffin the main stem of the lamp that transfers the fuel from the bowl to the mantle, vapourising it on the way tends to get slowly choked up. This obviously tends to reduce the light output of the lamp so something has to be done. With Tilleys this stem is quite a cheap item and really it is worth replacing it, and the needle that runs up the centre, once a year. With the larger lamps this item is rather expensive and therefore a good clean is the only answer. The carbon deposits can be scraped off the centre needle and the stem wiped out with a pipe cleaner or thin rag and thin rod. This is not perfect but at least it stops the deposits from building up to an unacceptable level.

Pressure lamps are, as I have said, simple devices but ones that need care and attention if you want them to give trouble free operation. Even if you do not want to take it apart at least brush it over and check its operation because as with everything else the moment it chooses to fail will just be the moment you don't want it to.

Index